COMMERCIAL POLITICS
(1837-1856)

LECTOR HOUSE PUBLIC DOMAIN WORKS

COMMERCIAL POLITICS (1837-1856)

RICHARD HENRY GRETTON,
SAMUEL EDWARD WINBOLT,
KENNETH NORMAN BELL

ISBN: 978-93-5614-392-0

Published: 1914

LECTOR HOUSE LLP
E-MAIL: lectorpublishing@gmail.com

BELL'S ENGLISH HISTORY SOURCE BOOKS

COMMERCIAL POLITICS
(1837-1856)

BY

R. H. GRETTON

FORMERLY DEMY OF MAGDALEN COLLEGE, OXFORD
AUTHOR OF "MODERN HISTORY OF THE ENGLISH PEOPLE"

General Editors: S. E. WINBOLT, M.A., and KENNETH BELL, M.A.

1914

CONTENTS

INTRODUCTION

This series of English History Source Books is intended for use with any ordinary textbook of English History. Experience has conclusively shown that such apparatus is a valuable—nay, an indispensable—adjunct to the history lesson. It is capable of two main uses: either by way of lively illustration at the close of a lesson, or by way of inference-drawing, before the textbook is read, at the beginning of the lesson. The kind of problems and exercises that may be based on the documents are legion, and are admirably illustrated in a *History of England for Schools*, Part I., by Keatinge and Frazer, pp. 377-381. However, we have no wish to prescribe for the teacher the manner in which he shall exercise his craft, but simply to provide him and his pupils with materials hitherto not readily accessible for school purposes. The very moderate price of the books in this series should bring them within the reach of every secondary school. Source books enable the pupil to take a more active part than hitherto in the history lesson. Here is the apparatus, the raw material: its use we leave to teacher and taught.

Our belief is that the books may profitably be used by all grades of historical students between the standards of fourth-form boys in secondary schools and undergraduates at Universities. What differentiates students at one extreme from those at the other is not so much the kind of subject-matter dealt with, as the amount they can read into or extract from it.

In regard to choice of subject-matter, while trying to satisfy the natural demand for certain "stock" documents of vital importance, we hope to introduce much fresh and novel matter. It is our intention that the majority of the extracts should be lively in style—that is, personal, or descriptive, or rhetorical, or even strongly partisan—and should not so much profess to give the truth as supply data for inference. We aim at the greatest possible variety, and lay under contribution letters, biographies, ballads and poems, diaries, debates, and newspaper accounts. Economics, London, municipal and social life generally, and local history, are represented in these pages.

The order of the extracts is strictly chronological, each being numbered, titled, and dated, and its authority given. The text is modernised, where necessary, to the extent of leaving no difficulties in reading.

We shall be most grateful to teachers and students who may send us suggestions for improvement.

S. E. WINBOLT.
KENNETH BELL.

NOTE TO THIS VOLUME

I acknowledge, with thanks, the permission of Mr. John Murray to reprint the extracts from *Queen Victoria's Letters* on pp. 26, 68, 84; and from *The Croker Papers* on p. 26; also the permission of Messrs. Longmans, Green and Co. to reprint the extracts from *The Greville Memoirs* on pp. 29, 68, 85; and those from *The Life of Lord John Russell* on pp. 99, 118.

R. H. G.

COMMERCIAL POLITICS (1837-1856)

ACCESSION OF QUEEN VICTORIA (1837).

Sybil

Source.—Lord Beaconsfield's *Sybil*, bk. i., chap. vi.

Hark! It tolls! All is over. The great bell of the metropolitan cathedral announces the death of the last son of George the Third who probably will ever reign in England. He was a good man: with feelings and sympathies; deficient in culture rather than ability; with a sense of duty; and with something of the conception of what should be the character of an English monarch. Peace to his manes! We are summoned to a different scene.

In a palace in a garden—not in a haughty keep, proud with the fame, but dark with the violence of ages; not in a regal pile, bright with the splendour, but soiled with the intrigues of courts and factions—in a palace in a garden, meet scene for youth, and innocence, and beauty—came a voice that told the maiden that she must ascend her throne!

The Council of England is summoned for the first time within her bowers. There are assembled the prelates and captains and chief men of her realm; the priests of the religion that consoles, the heroes of the sword that has conquered, the votaries of the craft that has decided the fate of empires; men grey with thought, and fame, and age; who are the stewards of divine mysteries, who have toiled in secret cabinets, who have encountered in battle the hosts of Europe, who have struggled in the less merciful strife of aspiring senates; men too, some of them, lords of a thousand vassals and chief proprietors of provinces, yet not one of them whose heart does not at this moment tremble as he awaits the first presence of the maiden who must now ascend her throne.

A hum of half-suppressed conversation which would attempt to conceal the excitement, which some of the greatest of them have since acknowledged, fills that brilliant assemblage; that sea of plumes, and glittering stars, and gorgeous dresses. Hush! The portals open. She comes. The silence is as deep as that of a noontide forest. Attended for a moment by her royal mother and the ladies of her court, who bow and then retire, VICTORIA ascends her throne; a girl, alone, and for the first time, amid an assemblage of men.

In a sweet and thrilling voice, and with a composed mien which indicates rather the absorbing sense of august duty than an absence of emotion, THE QUEEN announces her accession to the throne of her ancestors, and the humble hope that divine Providence will guard over the fulfilment of her lofty trust.

The prelates and captains and chief men of her realm then advance to the throne, and, kneeling before her, pledge their troth, and take the sacred oaths of allegiance and supremacy.

Allegiance to one who rules over the land that the great Macedonian could not conquer; and over a continent of which even Columbus never dreamed: to the Queen of every sea, and of nations in every zone.

It is not of these that I would speak; but of a nation nearer her footstool, which at this moment looks to her with anxiety, with affection, perhaps with hope. Fair and serene, she has the blood and beauty of the Saxon. Will it be her proud destiny at length to bear relief to suffering millions, and, with that soft hand which might inspire troubadours and guerdon knights, break the last links in the chain of Saxon thraldom?

AFFAIRS IN CANADA (1837).

Report by Lord Durham

Source.—*Report on the Affairs of British North America.* By Lord Durham. Printed for the House of Commons, 1839.

The lengthened and various discussions which had for some years been carried on between the contending parties in the Colony, and the representations which had been circulated at home, had produced in mine, as in most minds in England, a very erroneous view of the parties at issue in Lower Canada. The quarrel which I was sent to heal had been a quarrel between the executive government and the popular branch of the legislature. The latter body had, apparently, been contending for popular rights and free government. The executive government had been defending the prerogative of the Crown and the institutions which, in accordance with the principles of the British Constitution, had been established as checks on the unbridled exercise of popular power.... I expected to find a contest between a government and a people. I found two nations warring in the bosom of a single state; I found a struggle, not of principles, but of races; and I perceived that it would be idle to attempt any amelioration of laws or institutions until we could first succeed in terminating the deadly animosity that now separates the inhabitants of Lower Canada into the hostile divisions of French and English.... To conceive the incompatibility of the two races in Canada it is not enough that we should picture to ourselves a community composed of equal proportions of French and English. We must bear in mind what kind of French and English they are that are brought in contact, and in what proportions they meet.

The institutions of France during the period of the colonisation of Canada were, perhaps, more than those of any other nation, calculated to repress the intelligence and freedom of the great mass of the people. These institutions followed the Canadian colonist across the Atlantic. The same central, ill-organised, unimproving, and repressive despotism extended over him. Not merely was he allowed no voice in the government of his province or the choice of his rulers, but he was not even permitted to associate with his neighbours for the regulation of those municipal affairs which the central authority neglected under the pretext of managing. He obtained his land on a tenure singularly calculated to promote his immediate comfort and to check his desire to better his condition; he was placed at once in a life of constant and unvarying labour, of great material comfort, and feudal dependence. The ecclesiastical authority to which he had been accustomed established its institutions around him, and the priest continued to exercise over him his ancient influence. No general provision was made for education; and as its necessity was not appreciated, the colonist made no attempt to repair the negligence of his government. It need not surprise us that, under such circumstances, a race of men habituated to the incessant labour of a rude and unskilled agriculture, and habitually fond of social enjoyments, congregated together in rural communities, occupying portions of the wholly unappropriated soil, sufficient to provide each family with material comforts far beyond their ancient means, or almost their conceptions; that they made little advance beyond the first progress in comfort, which the bounty of the soil absolutely forced upon them; that under the same institutions they remained the same uninstructed, inactive, unprogressive people. Along the alluvial banks of the St. Lawrence and its tributaries they have cleared two or three strips of land, cultivated them in the worst method of small farming, and established a series of continuous villages, which give the country of the seignories the appearance of a never-ending street. Besides the cities which were the seats of government, no towns were established. The rude manufactures of the country were, and still are, carried on in the cottage by the family of the habitant; and an insignificant proportion of the population derived their subsistence from the scarcely discernible commerce of the province. The mass of the community exhibited in the New World the characteristics of the peasantry of Europe. Society was dense; and even the wants and the poverty which the pressure of population occasions in the Old World became not to be wholly unknown. They clung to ancient prejudices, ancient customs, and ancient laws, not from any strong sense of their beneficial effects, but with the unreasoning tenacity of an uneducated and unprogressive people. Nor were they wanting in the virtues of a simple and industrious life, or in those which common consent attributes to the nation from which they spring. The temptations which, in other states of society, lead to offences against property, and the passions which prompt to violence, were little known amongst them. They are mild and kindly, frugal, industrious, and honest, very sociable, cheerful, and hospitable, and distinguished for a courtesy and real politeness, which pervades every class of society. The conquest has changed them but little. The higher classes and the inhabitants of the towns have adopted some English customs and feelings, but the continued negligence of the British Government left the mass of the people without any of the institutions which would have elevated them in freedom and civilisation. It has left them without the education and without the institutions of local self-government that would have assimilated their character and habits, in the easiest and best way, to those of the Empire of which they became a part. They remain an old and stationary society in a new and progressive world.... The common opinion, however, that all classes of the Canadians are equally ignorant is perfectly erroneous. The piety and benevolence of the early possessors of the country founded in the seminaries that exist in different parts of the province institutions of which the funds and activity have long been directed to the promotion of education. Seminaries cond colleges have been by these bodies established in the cities and in other central points. The education given in these establishments greatly resembles the kind given in the English public schools, though it is rather more varied. It is entirely in the hands of the Catholic clergy. The number of pupils in these establishments is estimated altogether at about a thousand, and they turn out every year, as far as I could ascertain, between two and three hundred young men thus educated. Almost all of these are members of the family of some habitant.... Thus the persons of most education in every village belong to the same families and the same station in life as the illiterate habitants.... To this singular state of things I attribute the extraordinary influence of the Canadian demagogues. Over the class of persons by whom the peasantry are thus led the Government has not acquired, or ever laboured to acquire, influence; its members have been thrown into opposition by the system of exclusion long prevalent in the colony, and it is by their agency that the leaders of the Assembly have been enabled hitherto to move as one mass, in whatever direction they thought proper, the simple and ductile population of the country. The entire neglect of education by the Government has thus more than any other cause contributed to render the people ungovernable, and to invest the agitator with the power which he wields against the laws and the public tranquillity.

Among this people the progress of emigration has of late years introduced an English population exhibiting the characteristics with which we are familiar as those of the most enterprising of every class of our countrymen. The circumstances of the early colonial administration excluded the native Canadian from power, and vested all offices of trust and emolument in the hands of strangers of English origin. The highest posts in the law were confided to the same class of persons. The functionaries of the civil government, together with the officers of the army, composed a kind of privileged class, occupying the first place in the community, and excluding the higher class of the natives from society, as well as from the government of their own country. It was not till within a very few years, as was testified by persons who had seen much of the country, that this society of civil and military functionaries ceased to exhibit towards the higher order of Canadians an exclusiveness of demeanour which was more revolting to a sensitive and polite people than the monopoly of power and profit. Nor was this national favouritism discontinued until after repeated complaints and an angry contest, which had excited passions that concession could not allay. The races had become enemies ere a tardy justice was extorted; and even then the Government discovered a mode of distributing its patronage among the Canadians which was quite as offensive to that people as their previous exclusion:

It was not long after the conquest that another and larger class of English settlers began to enter the province. English capital was attracted to Canada by the vast quantity and valuable nature of the exportable produce of the country and the great facilities for commerce presented by the natural means of internal intercourse. The ancient trade of the country was conducted on a much larger and more profitable scale, and new branches of industry were explored. The active and regular habits of the English capitalist drove out of all the more profitable kinds of industry their inert and careless competitors of the French race; but in respect of the greater part (almost the whole) of the commerce and manufactures of the country the English cannot be said to have encroached on the French, for, in fact, they created employments and profits which had not previously existed.... The English farmer carried with him the experience and habits of the most improved agriculture in the world. He settled himself in the townships bordering on the seigniories, and brought a fresh soil and improved cultivation to compete with the worn-out and slovenly farm of the habitant. He often took the very farm which the Canadian settler had abandoned, and by superior management made that a source of profit which had only impoverished his predecessor. The ascendency which an unjust favouritism had contributed to give to the English race in the government and the legal profession, their own superior energy, skill, and capital secured to them in every branch of industry. They have developed the resources of the country; they have constructed or improved its means of communication; they have created its internal and foreign commerce. The entire wholesale and a large portion of the retail trade of the province, with the most profitable and flourishing farms, are now in the hands of this numerical minority of the population.... The two races thus distinct have been brought into the same community under circumstances which rendered their contact inevitably productive of collision. The difference of language from the first kept them asunder. It is not anywhere a virtue of the English race to look with complacency on any manners, customs, or laws which appear strange to them; accustomed to form a high estimate of their own superiority, they take no pains to conceal from others their contempt and intolerance of their usages. They found the French Canadians filled with an equal amount of national pride—a sensitive but inactive pride, which disposes that people not to resent insult, but rather to keep aloof from those who would keep them under. The French could not but feel the superiority of English enterprise; they could not shut their eyes to their success in every undertaking in which they came into contact and to the constant superiority which they were acquiring. They looked upon their rivals with alarm, with jealousy, and finally with hatred. The English repaid them with a scorn which soon also assumed the same form of hatred. The French complained of the arrogance and injustice of the English; the English accused the French of the vices of a weak and conquered people, and charged them with meanness and perfidy.

THE STATE OF ENGLAND (1838).

I. RURAL DISTRICTS.

Sybil

Source.—Lord Beaconsfield's *Sybil*, bk. ii., chap. iii.

The situation of the rural town of Marney was one of the most delightful easily to be imagined. In a spreading dale, contiguous to the margin of a clear and lively stream, surrounded by meadows and gardens and backed by lofty hills, undulating and richly wooded, the traveller on the opposite heights of the dale would often stop to admire the merry prospect, that recalled to him the traditional epithet of his country.

Beautiful illusion! For behind that laughing landscape penury and disease fed upon the vitals of a miserable population!

The contrast between the interior of the town and its external aspect was as striking as it was full of pain. With the exception of the dull high street, which had the usual characteristics of a small agricultural market town, some sombre mansions, a dingy inn, and a petty bourse, Marney mainly consisted of a variety of narrow and crowded lanes formed by cottages built of rubble, or unhewn stones without cement, and from age or badness of the material, looking as if they could scarcely hold together. The gaping chinks admitted every blast, the leaning chimneys had lost half their original height; the rotten rafters were evidently misplaced; while in many instances the thatch, yawning in some parts to admit the wind and wet, and in all utterly unfit for its original purpose of giving protection from the weather, looked more like the top of a dunghill than a cottage. Before the doors of these dwellings, and often surrounding them, ran open drains full of animal and vegetable refuse, decomposing into disease, or sometimes in their imperfect course filling foul pits or spreading into stagnant pools, while a concentrated solution of every species of dissolving filth was allowed to soak through and thoroughly impregnate the walls and ground adjoining.

These wretched tenements seldom consisted of more than two rooms, in one of which the whole family, however numerous, were obliged to sleep, without distinction of age, sex, or suffering.... The swarming walls had neither windows nor doors sufficient to keep out the weather, or admit the sun, or supply the means of ventilation; the humid and putrid roof of thatch exhaling malaria like all other decaying vegetable matter. The dwelling rooms were neither boarded nor paved....

This town of Marney was a metropolis of agricultural labour, for the proprietors of the neighbourhood having for the last half century acted on the system of destroying the cottages on their estates in order to become exempted from the maintenance of the population, the expelled people had flocked to Marney....

The eyes of this unhappy race might have been raised to the solitary spire that sprang up in the midst of them, the bearer of present consolation, the harbinger of future equality; but Holy Church at Marney had forgotten her sacred mission. We have introduced the reader to the vicar, an orderly man, who deemed he did his duty if he preached each week two sermons, and enforced humility on the congregation, and gratitude for the blessings of this life. The people of Marney took refuge in conventicles, which abounded; little plain buildings of pale brick, with the names painted on them of Sion, Bethel, Bethesda; names of a distant land, and the language of a persecuted and ancient race; yet such is the mysterious power of their divine quality, breathing consolation in the nineteenth century to the harassed forms and the harrowed souls of a Saxon peasantry.

But however devoted to his flock might have been the Vicar of Marney, his exertions for their well-being, under any circumstances, must have been mainly limited to spiritual consolation. Married and a father, he received for his labours the small tithes of the parish, which secured to him an income by no means equal to that of a superior banker's clerk, or the cook of a great loanmonger. The great tithes of Marney, which might be counted by thousands, swelled the vast rental which was drawn from this district by the fortunate earls that bore its name.

II. MINING DISTRICTS.

Sybil

Source. — Lord Beaconsfield's *Sybil*, bk. iii., chap, i.

The last rays of the sun, contending with clouds of smoke that drifted across the country, partially illumined a peculiar landscape. Far as the eye could reach— and the region was level, except where a range of limestone hills formed its distant limit—a wilderness of cottages, or tenements that were hardly entitled to a higher name, were scattered for many miles over the land; some detached, some connected in little rows, some clustering in groups, yet rarely forming continuous streets, but interspersed with blazing furnaces, heaps of burning coal, and piles of smouldering ironstone; while forges and engine chimneys roared and puffed in all directions, and indicated the frequent presence of the mouth of the mine and the bank of the coal-pit....

They come forth; the mine delivers its gang and the pit its bondmen; the forge is silent and the engine is still. The plain is covered with the swarming multitude: bands of stalwart men, broad-chested and muscular, wet with toil, and black as the children of the tropics; troops of youth—alas! of both sexes—though neither their raiment nor their language indicates the difference; all are clad in male attire; and oaths that men might shudder at issue from lips born to breathe words of sweetness. Yet these are to be—some are—the mothers of England! But can we wonder at the hideous coarseness of their language, when we remember the savage rudeness of their lives? Naked to the waist, an iron chain fastened to a belt of leather runs between their legs clad in canvas trousers, while on hands and feet an

English girl, for twelve, sometimes for sixteen, hours a day, hauls and hurries tubs of coal up subterranean roads, dark, precipitous, and plashy: circumstances that seem to have escaped the notice of the Society for the Abolition of Negro Slavery. Those worthy gentlemen, too, appear to have been singularly unconscious of the sufferings of the little Trappers, which was remarkable, as many of them were in their own employ.

See, too, these emerge from the bowels of the earth! Infants of four and five years of age, many of them girls, pretty and still soft and timid; entrusted with the fulfilment of most responsible duties, and the nature of which entails on them the necessity of being the earliest to enter the mine and the latest to leave it. Their labour indeed is not severe, for that would be impossible, but it is passed in darkness and in solitude. They endure that punishment which philosophical philanthropy has invented for the direst criminals, and which those criminals deem more terrible than the death for which it is substituted. Hour after hour elapses and all that reminds the infant Trappers of the world they have quitted and that which they have joined, is the passage of the coal-waggons for which they open the air-doors of the galleries, and on keeping which doors constantly closed, except at this moment of passage, the safety of the mine and the lives of the persons employed in it entirely depend.

III. FACTORY TOWNS.

Sybil, Coningsby

A.—**Source.**—Lord Beaconsfield's *Sybil*, bk. iii., chap. iv.

At the beginning of the revolutionary war, Wodgate was a sort of squatting district of the great mining region to which it was contiguous, a place where adventurers in the industry which was rapidly developing, settled themselves. It abounded in fuel which cost nothing, for though the veins were not worth working as a source of profit, the soil of Wodgate was similar in its superficial character to that of the country around. So a population gathered, and rapidly increased, in the ugliest spot in England, to which neither Nature nor art had contributed a single charm; where a tree could not be seen, a flower was unknown, where there was neither belfry nor steeple, nor a single sight that could soften the heart or humanise the mind.

Whatever may be the cause, whether, as not unlikely, the original squatters brought with them some traditionary skill, or whether their isolated and unchequered existence concentrated their energies on their craft, the fact is certain, that the inhabitants of Wodgate early acquired a celebrity as skilful workmen. As manufacturers of ironmongery they carry the palm from the whole district; as founders of brass and workers of steel, they fear none; while, as nailers and locksmiths, their fame has spread even to the European markets....

Here Labour reigns supreme. Its division indeed is favoured by their manners, but the interference or influence of mere capital is instantly resisted. The business of Wodgate is carried on by master workmen in their own houses, each of whom possesses an unlimited number of what they call apprentices, by whom their affairs are principally conducted, and whom they treat as the Mamlouks treated the Egyptians.

These master workmen, indeed, form a powerful aristocracy, nor is it possible to conceive one apparently more oppressive. They are ruthless tyrants; they habitually inflict upon their subjects punishments more grievous than the slave population of our colonies were ever visited with; not content with beating them with sticks or flogging them with knotted ropes, they are in the habit of felling them with hammers, or cutting their heads open with a file or lock. The most usual punishment, however, or rather stimulus to increase exertion, is to pull an apprentice's ears till they run with blood. These youths, too, are worked for sixteen and even twenty hours a day; they are often sold by one master to another; they are fed on carrion, and they sleep in lofts or cellars: yet, whether it be that they are hardened by brutality, and really unconscious of their degradation and unusual sufferings, or whether they are supported by the belief that their day to be masters and oppressors will surely arrive, the aristocracy of Wodgate is by no means so unpopular as the aristocracy of most other places.

In the first place it is a real aristocracy; it is privileged, but it does something for its privileges. It is distinguished from the main body not merely by name. It is the most knowing class at Wodgate; it possesses indeed in its way complete knowledge; and it imparts in its manner a certain quantity of it to those whom it guides. Thus it is an aristocracy that leads, and therefore a fact. Moreover, the social system of Wodgate is not an unvarying course of infinite toil. Their plan is to work hard, but not always. They seldom exceed four days of labour in the week. On Sunday the masters begin to drink; for the apprentices there is dog-fighting without any stint. On Monday and Tuesday the whole population of Wodgate is drunk; of all stations, ages, and sexes; even babes, who should be at the breast; for they are drammed with Godfrey's cordial. Here is relaxation, excitement; if less vice otherwise than might be at first anticipated, we must remember that excesses are checked by poverty of blood and constant exhaustion. Scanty food and hard labour are in their way, if not exactly moralists, a tolerably good police.

There are no others at Wodgate to preach or to control. It is not that the people are immoral, for immorality implies some forethought; or ignorant, for ignorance is relative; but they are animals; unconscious; their minds a blank; and their worst actions only the impulse of a gross or savage instinct. There are many in this town who are ignorant of their very names; very few who can spell them. It is rare that you meet with a young person who knows his own age; rarer to find the boy who has seen a book, or the girl who has seen a flower. Ask them the name of their sovereign, and they will give you an unmeaning stare; ask them the name of their religion, and they will laugh: who rules them on earth, or who can save them in heaven, are alike mysteries to them.

Wodgate had the appearance of a vast squalid suburb. As you advanced, leaving behind you long lines of little dingy tenements, with infants lying about the road, you expected every moment to emerge into some streets and encounter buildings bearing some correspondence in their size and comfort to the considerable population swarming and busied about you. Nothing of the kind. There were no public buildings of any sort; no churches, chapels, town-hall, institute, theatre; and the principal streets in the heart of the town in which were situate the coarse and grimy shops, though formed by houses of a greater elevation than the preceding, were equally narrow and, if possible, more dirty. At every fourth or fifth house, alleys seldom above a yard wide and streaming with filth, opened out of the street. These were crowded with dwellings of various size, while from the principal court often branched out a number of smaller alleys or rather narrow passages, than which nothing can be conceived more close and squalid and obscure. Here, during the days of business, the sound of the hammer and the file never cease, amid gutters of abomination and piles of foulness and stagnant pools of filth; reservoirs of leprosy and plague, whose exhalations were sufficient to taint the atmosphere of the whole kingdom and fill the country with fever and pestilence.

B.—**Source.**—Lord Beaconsfield's *Coningsby*, bk. iv., chap. ii.

He had travelled the whole day through the great district of labour, his mind excited by strange sights, and at length wearied by their multiplication. He had passed over the plains where iron and coal supersede turf and corn, dingy as the entrance to Hades, and flaming with furnaces; and now he was among illumined factories with more windows than Italian palaces, and smoking chimneys taller than Egyptian obelisks....

He entered chambers vaster than are told of in Arabian fable, and peopled with inhabitants more wonderful than Afrite or Peri. For there he beheld, in long continued ranks, those mysterious forms full of existence without life, that perform with facility and in an instant, what man can fulfil only with difficulty and in days. A machine is a slave that neither brings nor bears degradation; it is a being endowed with the greatest degree of energy and acting under the greatest degree of excitement, yet free at the same time from all passion and emotion. He is therefore not only a slave, but a supernatural slave. And why should one say that the machine does not live? It breathes, for its breath forms the atmosphere of some towns. It moves with more regularity than man. And has it not a voice? Does not the spindle sing like a merry girl at her work, and the steam engine roar in jolly chorus like a strong artisan handling his lusty tools, and gaining a fair day's wages for a fair day's toil?

Nor should the weaving-room be forgotten, where a thousand or fifteen hundred girls may be observed in their coral necklaces working like Penelope in the day-time; some pretty, some pert, some graceful and jocund, some absorbed in their occupation; a little serious some, few sad. And the cotton you have observed in its rude state, that you have seen the silent spinner change into thread and the bustling weaver convert into cloth, you may now watch, as in a moment it is tinted with beautiful colours, or printed with fanciful patterns. And yet the mystery of mysteries is to view machines making machines; a spectacle that fills the mind with curious, even awful, speculation.

From early morn to the late twilight, our Coningsby for several days devoted himself to the comprehension of Manchester. It was to him a new world pregnant with new ideas, and suggestive of new trains of thought and feeling. In this unprecedented partnership between capital and science, working on a spot which Nature had indicated as the fitting theatre of their exploits, he beheld a great source of the wealth of nations which had been reserved for these times, and he perceived that this wealth was rapidly developing classes whose power was very imperfectly recognised in the constitutional scheme, and whose duties in the social system seemed altogether omitted.

IRELAND AND HER LANDLORDS (1838).

Life of Thos. Drummond

Source.—R. Barry O'Brien's *Life and Letters of Thomas Drummond*, p. 273. (London: 1889.)

A.—*The Tipperary Magistrates to the Lord Lieutenant. Cashel, April 7, 1838.*

We, the undersigned magistrates of the County of Tipperary, this day assembled at Cashel, at a very short notice, beg leave respectfully to state to your Excellency, that it is with feelings of the deepest horror we communicate to your Excellency the dreadful and atrocious attack made by some villains upon the lives of Samuel Cooper, Esq., J.P., Austin Cooper, Esq., and Francis Wayland, Esq., on the 5th day of April.

It appears that these gentlemen were proceeding to the fair of Tipperary on that day, the two Mr. Coopers in a gig, and Mr. Wayland on horseback, when they were fired upon by four men. Mr. Samuel Cooper and Mr. Wayland returned the fire, but it is horrifying to relate that Mr. Austin Cooper was shot dead by a ball passing through his head, and Mr. Wayland was severely wounded in the hip....

We, the undersigned, declare that in that district neither life nor property is safe. We therefore respectfully trust that your Excellency will put in force the strongest powers which the laws of the land permit in those districts.

We consider it our duty to state to your Excellency that we believe the result of the late assizes for this county has proved how terrible is the state of intimidation which exists, or seems to exist, among the juries of this county....

We beg leave respectfully to hope that Her Majesty's Government will bring in a Bill to Parliament for the purpose of inflicting a heavier penalty than that now in force on persons for having unregistered arms or ammunition in their possession.

B.—*Drummond to the Tipperary Magistrates. Dublin Castle, May 22, 1838.*

My lord,—In the communication of the 18th of April, which I had the honour to make to your Lordship by command of the Lord Lieutenant, your Lordship was informed that His Excellency considered it necessary to institute an immediate and careful inquiry....

His Excellency deemed it his duty to direct, among other inquiries, letters to be addressed to the several stipendiary magistrates of the county, calling upon them to state whether any and what instances of injury to the persons or property of jurors had come under their observation, which could be distinctly attributed to the verdicts given by such jurors. In the answers received from all these gentlemen, they uniformly declare that not a single instance of the kind has ever occurred to their knowledge....

His Excellency has also obtained a return of the several juries at the last assizes of Tipperary, and he finds that the great majority of jurors resided in towns, chiefly in Clonmel, and therefore were not likely to be influenced by apprehensions of danger to person or property; and further, on examining the list, it has been found that, of the hundred jurors who constituted the juries in the several cases of homicide, fifty-two served both on convicting and acquitting juries, thirty on convicting juries only, and eighteen only on acquitting juries.

His Excellency also felt it his duty to refer the statement of the memorialists to the judge who presided at the last assizes, and His Excellency has received a reply from that learned person, of which the following is an extract:

"It did not appear to me that there existed any grounds, either of facts or inference, for apprehending that the juries were intimidated; on the contrary, I considered they discharged their duties free from any bias arising from personal apprehension, or any other cause; and with regard to their verdicts, they uniformly received and acted upon the legal character of the crime as laid down by the Court, at the same time exercising their own judgments, as in their exclusive province, upon the credit to which they considered the witnesses were entitled...."

The Government has been at all times ready to afford the utmost aid in its power to suppress disturbance and crime, and its efforts have been successful, so far as regards open violations of the law. Faction fights and riots at fairs, which were generally of a very ferocious character and the fruitful source of much subsequent crime, have been to a very great degree suppressed, though heretofore most commonly suffered to pass unchecked and unpunished; but there are certain classes of crime, originating in other causes, which are much more difficult of repression. The utmost exertion of vigilance and precaution cannot always effectually guard against them, and it becomes of importance to consider the causes which have led to a state of society so much to be deplored, with a view to ascertain whether any corrective means are in the immediate power of the Government or the Legislature. When the character of the great majority of serious outrages occurring in many parts of Ireland, though unhappily most frequent in Tipperary, is considered, it is impossible to doubt that the causes from which they mainly spring are connected with the tenure and occupation of land. But His Excellency feels that it would be quite beyond the limits, and not consistent with the character of a communication of this nature, either to enter into an examination of the lamentably destitute condition of a cottier tenantry, possessing no adequate means of continuous support, or to advert in detail to the objects for which the formation of such a class was originally either permitted or directly encouraged. If from political changes or the improvements in modern husbandry these objects are not any longer to be attained by the continuance of such a state of things, His Excellency conceives that it may become matter of serious question whether the proprietors of the soil are not in many instances attempting too rapidly to retrace their steps when he finds the fact to be, from returns furnished by the Clerk of the Peace for Tipperary, that the number of ejectments in 1837 is not less than double the number in 1833. The deficiency of a demand for labour, and the want, as yet, of any legal provision against utter destitution, leave this humble class, when ejected, without any certain provision against actual starvation. Hence the wholesale expulsion of cottier tenants is unfortunately found with the great body of the people to enlist the strongest feelings—those of self-preservation—on the side even of guilt, in vindication of what they falsely assume to be their rights; and hence a sympathy for persons charged with crimes supposed to have arisen from those causes, is still found a lamentable exception to that increased general respect for the laws which has of late years been remarked with satisfaction by those concerned in the administration of justice.

Property has its duties as well as its rights. To the neglect of those duties in times past is mainly to be ascribed that diseased state of society in which such crimes take their rise; and it is not in the enactment or enforcement of statutes of extraordinary severity, but chiefly in the better and more faithful performance of those duties, and the more enlightened and humane exercise of those rights, that a permanent remedy for such disorders is to be sought....

THE CHARTER OF COLONIAL SELF-GOVERNMENT (1839).

Report by Lord Durham

Source.—*Report on the Affairs of British North America.* By Lord Durham.
Printed for the House of Commons, 1839.

Such are the lamentable results of the political and social evils which have so long agitated the Canadas, and such is their condition, that at the present moment we are called on to take immediate precautions against dangers so alarming as those of rebellion, foreign invasion, and utter exhaustion and depopulation. When I look on the various and deep-rooted causes of mischief which the past inquiry has pointed out as existing in every institution, in the constitutions, and in the very composition of society throughout a great part of these provinces, I almost shrink from the apparent presumption of grappling with these gigantic difficulties. Nor shall I attempt to do so in detail. I rely on the efficacy of reform in the constitutional system by which these colonies are governed, for the removal of every abuse in their administration which defective institutions have engendered. If a system can be devised which shall lay in these countries the foundation of an efficient and popular government, ensure harmony, in place of collision, between the various powers of the State, and bring the influence of a vigorous public opinion to bear on every detail of public affairs, we may rely on sufficient remedies being found for the present vices of the administrative system.

It is not by weakening but strengthening the influence of the people on its government; by confining within much narrower bounds than those hitherto allotted to it, and not by extending the interference of the Imperial authorities in the details of colonial affairs, that I believe that harmony is to be restored where dissension has so long prevailed, and a regularity and vigour hitherto unknown introduced into the administration of these Provinces. It needs no change in the principles of government, no invention of a new constitutional theory, to supply the remedy which would, in my opinion, completely remove the existing political disorders. It needs but to follow out consistently the principles of the British Constitution, and introduce into the government of these great Colonies those wise provisions, by which alone the working of the representative system can in any country be rendered harmonious and efficient. We are not now to consider the policy of establishing representative government in the North American Colonies. That has been irrevocably done, and the experiment of depriving the people of their present constitutional power is not to be thought of. To conduct their Government harmoniously, in accordance with its established principles, is now the business of its rulers, and I know not how it is possible to secure that harmony in any other way than by administering the Government on those principles which have been found perfectly efficacious in Great Britain. I would not impair a single prerogative of the Crown; on the contrary, I believe that the interests of the people of these Colonies require the protection of prerogatives which have not hitherto been exercised. But the Crown must, on the other hand, submit to the necessary consequences of representative institutions; and if it has to carry on the Government in unison with a representative body, it must consent to carry it on by means of those in whom that representative body has confidence.

In England this principle has so long been considered an indisputable and essential part of our constitution that it has really hardly ever been found necessary to inquire into the means by which its observance is enforced. When a Ministry ceases to command a majority in Parliament on great questions or policy, its doom is immediately sealed; and it would appear to us as strange to attempt for any time to carry on a Government by means of ministers perpetually in a minority, as it would be to pass laws with a majority of votes against them.... If Colonial Legislatures have frequently stopped the supplies, if they have harassed public servants by unjust or harsh impeachments, it was because the removal of an unpopular administration could not be effected in the Colonies by those milder indications of a want of confidence which have always sufficed to attain the end in the mother country.

The means which have occasionally been proposed in the Colonies themselves appear to me by no means calculated to attain the desired end in the best way. An elective executive council would not only be utterly inconsistent with monarchical government, but would really, under the nominal authority of the Crown, deprive the community of one of the great advantages of an hereditary monarchy. Every purpose of popular control might be combined with every advantage of vesting the immediate choice of advisers in the Crown, were the Colonial Governor to be instructed to secure the co-operation of the Assembly in his policy, by entrusting its administration to such men as could command a majority; and if he were given to understand that he need count on no aid from home in any difference with the Assembly, that should not directly involve the relations between the mother country and the Colony....

I know that it has been urged that the principles which are productive of harmony and good government in the mother country, are by no means applicable to a colonial dependency. It is said that it is necessary that the administration of a colony should be carried on by persons nominated without any reference to the wishes of its people; that they have to carry into effect the policy, not of that people, but of the authorities at home; and that a colony which should name all its own administrative functionaries, would, in fact, cease to be dependent. I admit that the system which I propose would, in fact, place the internal government of the colony in the hands of the colonists themselves; and that we should thus leave to them the execution of the laws, of which we have long entrusted the making solely to them. Perfectly aware of the value of our colonial possessions, and strongly impressed with the necessity of maintaining our connexion with them, I know not in what respect it can be desirable that we should interfere with their internal legislation in matters which do not affect their relations with the mother country. The matters which so concern us are very few. The constitution of the form of government—the regulation of foreign relations, and of trade with the mother country, the other British Colonies, and foreign nations—and the disposal of the public lands, are the only points on which the mother country requires a control. This control is now sufficiently secured by the authority of the Imperial Legislature; by the protection which the colony derives from us against foreign enemies; by the beneficial terms which our laws secure to its trade; and by its share of the reciprocal benefits which would be conferred by a wise system of colonization. A perfect subordination, on the part of the Colony, on these points, is secured by the advantages which it finds in the continuance of its connexion with the Empire. It certainly is not strengthened, but greatly weakened, by a vexatious interference on the part of the Home Government, with the enactment of laws for regulating the internal concerns of the Colony, or in the selection of the persons entrusted with their execution. The colonists may not always know what laws are best for them, or which of their countrymen are the fittest for conducting their affairs; but, at least, they have a greater interest in coming to a right judgment on these points, and will take greater pains to do so than those whose welfare is very remotely and slightly affected by the good or bad legislation of these portions of the Empire. If the colonists make bad laws, and select improper persons to conduct their affairs, they will generally be the only, always the greatest, sufferers; and, like the people of other countries, they must bear the ills which they bring on themselves, until they choose to apply the remedy. But it surely cannot be the duty or the interest of Great Britain to keep a most expensive military possession of these Colonies, in order that a Governor or Secretary of State may be able to confer colonial appointments on one rather than another set of persons in the Colonies.

> (Lord Durham went on to assert that it was essential to his scheme that the government of the colony should be British, and that the numerical superiority of the French in Lower Canada could most peaceably be remedied by legislative union of the Provinces of Upper and Lower Canada, which would give an English majority; and he proceeds:)

I am inclined to go further, and inquire whether all these objects would not more surely be attained by extending this legislative union over all the British Provinces in North America; and whether the advantages which I anticipate for two of them, might not, and should not in justice be extended over all. Such an union would at once decisively settle the question of races; it would enable all the Provinces to co-operate for all common purposes; and, above all, it would form a great and powerful people, possessing the means of securing good and responsible government for itself, and which, under the protection of the British Empire, might in some measure counterbalance the preponderant and increasing influence of the United States on the American continent. I do not anticipate that a Colonial Legislature thus strong and thus self-governing would desire to abandon the connexion with Great Britain. On the contrary, I believe that the practical relief from undue interference, which would be the result of such a change, would strengthen the present bond of feelings and interests; and that the connexion would become more durable and advantageous, by having more of equality, of freedom, and of local independence. But at any rate, our first duty is to secure the well-being of our colonial countrymen; and if in the hidden decrees of that wisdom by which this world is ruled it is written that these countries are not for ever to remain portions of the Empire, we owe it to our honour to take good care that, when they separate from us, they should not be the only countries on the American continent in which the Anglo-Saxon race shall be found unfit to govern itself.

I am in truth so far from believing that the increased power and weight that would be given to these Colonies by union would endanger their connexion with the Empire, that I look to it as the only means of fostering such a national feeling throughout them as would effectually counterbalance whatever tendencies may now exist towards separation. No large community of free and intelligent men will long feel contented with a political system which places them, because it places their country, in a position of inferiority to their neighbours. The colonist of Great Britain is linked, it is true, to a mighty Empire; and the glories of its history, the visible signs of its present power, and the civilisation of its people, are calculated to raise and gratify his national pride. But he feels also that his link to that Empire is one of remote dependence; he catches but passing and inadequate glimpses of its power and prosperity; he knows that in its government he and his own countrymen have no voice. While his neighbour on the other side of the frontier assumes importance, from the notion that his vote exercises some influence on the councils, and that he himself has some share in the progress, of a mighty nation, the colonist feels the deadening influence of the narrow and subordinate community to which he belongs.... If we wish to prevent the extension of this influence, it can only be done by raising up for the colonist some nationality of his own; by elevating these small and unimportant communities into a society having some objects of a national importance; and by thus giving their inhabitants a country which they will be unwilling to see absorbed even into one more powerful.

While I believe that the establishment of a comprehensive system of government, and of an effectual union between the different Provinces, would produce this important effect on the feelings of their inhabitants, I am inclined to attach very great importance to the influence which it would have in giving greater scope and satisfaction to the legitimate ambition of the most active and prominent persons to be found in them. If, as it is commonly asserted, the disorders of these colonies have, in great measure, been fomented by the influence of designing and ambitious individuals, this evil will best be remedied by allowing such a scope for the desires of such men as shall direct their ambition into the legitimate channel of furthering, and not of thwarting, their Government. By creating high prizes in a general and responsible Government, we shall immediately afford the means of pacifying the turbulent ambitions, and of employing in worthy and noble occupations the talents which now are only exerted to foment disorder.

THE BEDCHAMBER PLOT (1839).

Queen Victoria's Letters and The Croker Papers

I. THE QUEEN AND LORD MELBOURNE.

Source.—*Letters of Queen Victoria*: 1837-1861, vol. i., p. 204.(London: 1907.)

A.—*Viscount Melbourne to Queen Victoria. May 9, 1839.*

Lord Melbourne presents his humble duty to your Majesty, and begs to suggest that if Sir Robert Peel presses for the dismissal of those of your Household who are not in Parliament, you may observe that in so doing he is pressing your Majesty more hardly than any Minister ever pressed a Sovereign before.

When the Government was changed in 1830, the principal posts of the Household were placed at the disposal of Lord Grey, but the Grooms and Equerries were not removed.

When Sir Robert Peel himself became Minister in 1834, no part of the Household were removed except those who were in Parliament.

When I became Prime Minister again in 1835, none of the Grooms or Equerries were removed because none of them were in Parliament.

They press upon your Majesty, whose personal feelings ought from your circumstances to be more consulted, a measure which no Minister before ever pressed upon a Sovereign.

If this is put to him by your Majesty, Lord Melbourne does not see how he can resist it.

B.—*Queen Victoria to Viscount Melbourne. Buckingham Palace, May 9, 1839.*

The Queen writes one line to prepare Lord Melbourne for what *may* happen in a very few hours. Sir Robert Peel has behaved very ill, and has insisted on my giving up my Ladies, to which I replied that I never would consent, and I never saw a man so frightened. He said he must go to the Duke of Wellington and consult with him, when both would return, and he said this must suspend all further proceedings, and he asked whether I should be ready to receive a decision, which I said I should; he was quite perturbed—but this is *infamous*. I said, besides many other things, that if he or the Duke of Wellington had been at the head of the Government when I came to the Throne, perhaps there might have been a few more Tory Ladies, but that then if you had come in Office you would never have *dreamt* of changing them. I was calm but very decided, and I think you would have been pleased to see my composure and great firmness; the Queen of England will not submit to such trickery. Keep yourself in readiness, for you may soon be wanted.

C.—*Viscount Melbourne to Queen Victoria. May 9, 1839.*

Lord Melbourne presents his humble duty to your Majesty. This is a matter of so much importance, and may have such grave results, that any advice which Lord Melbourne could give would be of little importance unless it coincided with the opinions of others, and particularly of all those who were and intend still to continue to be his colleagues.

It will depend upon their determination whether your Majesty is to be supported or not. The best course will perhaps be that you should have Sir Robert Peel's determination, say nothing, but send for Lord Melbourne, and lay the matter before him. Lord Melbourne will then summon a Cabinet to consider of it.

II. THE TORY SIDE OF IT.

A.—**Source.**—*The Croker Papers*, vol. ii., p. 346. (London: 1884.)

J. W. Croker to the King of Hanover. May 11.

The mission of Sir Robert Peel failed upon what I may call an abstract principle—the right of the Minister to interfere at all in the female household. No lady's name was mentioned by Sir Robert, for on his saying to the Queen, "As to ladies of the household" her Majesty is said to have interrupted him at once by saying: "Oh, I do not mean to make any change among them." This is the sum of the whole affair. Sir Robert Peel could not admit the broad principle that all were to remain. Lady Normanby (whom the Queen particularly wishes for), for instance, the wife of the very Minister whose measures have been the cause of the change, two sisters of Lord Morpeth, the sisters-in-law of Lord John Russell, the daughter of the Privy Seal and Chancellor of the Exchequer. Your Majesty sees that though Sir Robert might, and I have no doubt would, have left the great body of the female attendants, he could not possibly have submitted to have the hostile party thus in possession of the personal favour, friendship, and confidence of the Queen. The general opinion is that this scheme was prepared even before the resignation, and that the whole has been a trick, though for my part I cannot see how it betters the position of the Whigs....

Her Majesty's ball last night was, I am told, rather dull, though she herself seemed in high spirits, as if she were pleased at retaining her Ministers.

B.—**Source.**—*The Greville Memoirs*: 1837-1852, vol. i., p. 208. (London: 1885.)

It is a high trial to our institutions when the wishes of a Princess of nineteen can overturn a great Ministerial combination, and when the most momentous matters of Government and legislation are influenced by her pleasure about the ladies of the Bedchamber.... The origin of the present mischief may be found in the objectionable composition of the Royal Household at the Accession. The Queen knew nobody, and was ready to take any ladies that Melbourne recommended to her. He ought to have taken care that the female part of her household should not have a political complexion, instead of making it exclusively Whig, as, unfortunately for her, he did; nor is it little matter of wonder that Melbourne should have consented to support her in such a case, and that he and his colleagues should have consented to act the strange, anomalous, unconstitutional part they have done.... To have met as a Cabinet, and to have advised her what answer to send to the man who still held her commission for forming a Government upon points relating to its formation, is utterly anomalous and unprecedented.

THE QUEEN'S MARRIAGE (1840).

Greville Memoirs

I. THE WEDDING DAY.

Source.—*The Greville Memoirs*: 1837-1852, vol. i., p. 266.

The wedding on Monday went off tolerably well. The week before was fine, and Albert drove about the town with a mob shouting at his heels. Tuesday, Wednesday, and to-day were all beautiful days, but Monday, as if by a malignant influence, was a dreadful day—torrents of rain and violent gusts of wind. Nevertheless a countless multitude thronged the park, and was scattered all over the town. I never beheld such a congregation as there was, in spite of the weather. The Queen proceeded in state from Buckingham Palace to St. James's without any cheering, but then it was raining enough to damp warmer loyalty than that of a London mob. The procession in the Palace was pretty enough by all accounts. Upon leaving the Palace for Windsor she and her young husband were pretty well received; but they went off in very poor and shabby style. Instead of the new chariot in which most married people are accustomed to dash along, they were in one of the old travelling coaches, the postillions in undress liveries, and with a small escort, three other coaches with post-horses following. The crowds on the road were so great that they did not reach the Castle till eight o'clock.

II. THE PRINCE CONSORT'S POSITION.

Source.—Sir Theodore Martin's *The Life of the Prince Consort*, vol. i., p. 69.
(London: 1875.)

Amid the general enthusiasm with which Prince Albert was welcomed in England, murmurs of jealousy and distrust were certain to be heard. There were some who, on purely selfish grounds, deprecated the marriage of the Queen with any but an English Prince; others who then, and for many years afterwards, were eager to surmise danger in the influence of a foreign prince upon the councils of the Crown. But the real difficulty of his task, being what he was by nature, and by the deliberate purpose which he had set before himself, lay elsewhere....

Although the husband of the Queen, the law—to use Her Majesty's words—took cognisance of him as "merely the younger son of the Duke of Coburg." Thus, while ostensibly occupying the most brilliant position in the kingdom, his right of precedence was to be disputed, and was disputed by a few members of the Royal Family, who made no secret of their disappointment that Her Majesty's choice had not fallen upon some scion of the reigning House in whom they had a nearer interest. A more pressing source of disquietude, however, existed in the fact that the Prince possessed no independent authority by right of his position, and could exercise none, even within his own household, without trenching upon the privileges of others, who were not always disposed to admit of interference....

Not less delicate was the Prince's task in fixing the line to be taken by him with regard to public affairs.... From the first, however, the Prince appreciated the extreme delicacy of his position, and laid down for himself the rule that no act of his should by possibility expose him to the imputation of interference with the machinery of the State, or of encroachment on the functions and privileges of the Sovereign.... The principle upon which he acted, as expressed by himself ten years later, in his letter to the Duke of Wellington, declining to entertain the offer of the command of the Army, cannot be too clearly kept in view in reading the story of his life. It was "to sink his own individual existence in that of his wife—to aim at no power by himself or for himself—to shun all ostentation—to assume no separate responsibility before the public—to make his position entirely a part of hers—to fill up every gap which, as a woman, she would naturally leave in the exercise of her regal functions—continually and anxiously to watch every part of the public business, in order to be able to advise and assist her at any moment in any of the multifarious and difficult questions brought before her—political, or social, or personal—to place all his powers at her command as the natural head of her family, superintendent of her household, manager of her private affairs, her sole confidential adviser in politics, and only assistant in her communications with the officers of the Government, her private secretary, and permanent minister."

THE CHARTIST PETITION (1842).

Hansard

Source.—*Hansard*, Third Series, lxii., col. 1373, Monday, May 2.

[A Petition from the working classes throughout the kingdom, of the presentation of which Mr. Thomas Duncombe had previously given notice, was brought down to the House, by a procession consisting of a vast multitude. Its bulk was so great, that the doors were not wide enough to admit it, and it was necessary to unroll it, to carry it into the House. When unrolled, it spread over a great part of the floor, and rose above the level of the table.]

Mr. Duncombe in presenting the petition gave the following statistics of signatures:

Manchester, 99,680; Newcastle and districts, 92,000; Glasgow and Lanarkshire, 78,062; Halifax, 36,400; Nottingham, 40,000; Leeds, 41,000; Birmingham, 43,000; Norwich, 21,560; Bolton, 18,500; Leicester, 18,000; Rochdale, 19,600; Loughborough and districts, 10,000; Salford, 19,600; East Riding, Yorkshire, agricultural districts, 14,840; Worcester, 10,000; Merthyr Tydvil and districts, 13,900; Aberdeen, 17,600; Keithly, 11,000; Brighton, 12,700; Bristol, 12,800; Huddersfield, 23,180; Sheffield, 27,200; Scotland, West Midland districts, 18,000; Dunfermline, 16,000; Cheltenham, 10,400; Liverpool, 23,000; Stalybridge and districts, 10,000; Stockport, 14,000; Macclesfield and suburbs, 10,000; North Lancashire, 52,000; Oldham, 15,000; Ashton, 14,200; Bradford and district, Yorkshire, 45,100; Burnley and district, 14,000; Preston and district, 24,000; Wigan, 10,000; London and suburbs, 200,000; from 371 other towns, villages, etc., 2,154,807. Total, 3,315,752.

The Petition was read, as follows:

To the honourable the Commons of Great Britain and Ireland, in Parliament assembled.

The petition of the undersigned people of the United Kingdom,

Sheweth—That Government originated from, was designed to protect the freedom and promote the happiness of, and ought to be responsible to, the whole people.

That the only authority on which any body of men can make laws and govern society, is delegation from the people.

That as Government was designed for the benefit and protection of, and must be obeyed and supported by, all, therefore all should be equally represented.

That any form of Government which fails to effect the purposes for which it was designed, and does not fully and completely represent the whole people, who are compelled to pay taxes to its support and obey the laws resolved upon by it, is unconstitutional, tyrannical, and ought to be amended or resisted.

That your honourable House, as at present constituted, has not been elected by, and acts irresponsibly of, the people; and hitherto has only represented parties, and benefited the few, regardless of the miseries, grievances, and petitions of the many. Your honourable House has enacted laws contrary to the expressed wishes of the people, and by unconstitutional means enforced obedience to them, thereby creating an unbearable despotism on the one hand, and degrading slavery on the other.

That if your honourable House is of opinion that the people of Great Britain and Ireland ought not to be fully represented, your petitioners pray that such opinion may be unequivocally made known, that the people may fully understand what they can or cannot expect from your honourable House; because if such be the decision of your honourable House, your petitioners are of opinion that where representation is denied, taxation ought to be resisted.

That your petitioners instance, in proof of their assertion, that your honourable House has not been elected by the people; that the population of Great Britain and Ireland is at the present time about twenty-six millions of persons; and that yet, out of this number, little more than nine hundred thousand have been permitted to vote in the recent election of representatives to make laws to govern the whole.

That the existing state of representation is not only extremely limited and unjust, but unequally divided, and gives preponderating influence to the landed and monied interests to the utter ruin of the small-trading and labouring classes.

That the borough of Guildford, with a population of 3,920 returns to Parliament as many members as the Tower Hamlets, with a population of 300,000; Evesham, with a population of 3,998, elects as many representatives as Manchester, with a population of 200,000; and Buckingham, Evesham, Totness, Guildford, Honiton, and Bridport, with a total population of 23,000, return as many representatives as Manchester, Finsbury, Tower Hamlets, Liverpool, Marylebone, and Lambeth, with a population of 1,400,000! these being but a very few instances of the enormous inequalities existing in what is called the representation of this country.

That bribery, intimidation, corruption, perjury, and riot, prevail at all parliamentary elections, to an extent best understood by the Members of your honourable House.

That your petitioners complain that they are enormously taxed to pay the interest of what is termed the national debt, a debt amounting at present to £800,000,000, being only a portion of the enormous amount expended in cruel and expensive wars for the suppression of all liberty, by men not authorised by the people, and who, consequently, had not right to tax posterity for the outrages committed by them upon mankind. And your petitioners loudly complain of the augmentation of that debt, after twenty-six years of almost uninterrupted peace, and whilst poverty and discontent rage over the land.

That taxation, both general and local, is at this time too enormous to be borne; and in the opinion of your petitioners is contrary to the spirit of the Bill of Rights, wherein it is clearly expressed that no subject shall be compelled to contribute to any tax, talliage, or aid, unless imposed by common consent in Parliament.

That in England, Ireland, Scotland, and Wales thousands of people are dying from actual want; and your petitioners, whilst sensible that poverty is the great existing cause of crime, view with mingled astonishment and alarm the ill-provision made for the poor, the aged, and infirm; and likewise perceive, with feelings of indignation, the determination of your honourable House to continue the Poor Law Bill in operation, notwithstanding the many proofs which have been afforded by sad experience of the unconstitutional principle of that Bill, of its unchristian character, and of the cruel and murderous effects produced upon the wages of working men and the lives of the subjects of this realm.

That your petitioners conceive that Bill to be contrary to all previous statutes, opposed to the spirit of the Constitution, and an actual violation of the precepts of the Christian religion; and therefore your petitioners look with apprehension to the results which may flow from its continuance.

That your petitioners would direct the attention of your honourable House to the great disparity existing between the wages of the producing millions and the salaries of those whose comparative usefulness ought to be questioned, where riches and luxury prevail amongst the rulers and poverty and starvation amongst the ruled.

That your petitioners, with all due respect and loyalty, would compare the daily income of the Sovereign Majesty with that of thousands of the working men of this nation; and whilst your petitioners have learned that her Majesty receives daily for her private use the sum of £164 17s. 10d., they have also ascertained that many thousands of the families of the labourers are only in the receipt of 3-¾d. per head per day.

That your petitioners have also learned that his royal Highness Prince Albert receives each day the sum of £104 2s., whilst thousands have to exist upon 3d. per head per day.

That your petitioners have also heard with astonishment that the King of Hanover daily receives £57 10s., whilst thousands of the tax-payers of this Empire live upon 2-¾d. per head per day.

That your petitioners have, with pain and regret, also learned that the Archbishop of Canterbury is daily in the receipt of £52 10s. per day, whilst thousands of the poor have to maintain their families upon an income not exceeding 2d. per head per day.

That, notwithstanding the wretched and unparalleled condition of the people, your honourable House has manifested no disposition to curtail the expenses of the State, to diminish taxation, or promote general prosperity.

That unless immediate remedial measures be adopted, your petitioners fear the increasing distress of the people will lead to results fearful to contemplate; because your petitioners can produce evidence of the gradual decline of wages, at the same time that the constant increase of the national burdens must be apparent to all.

That your petitioners know that it is the undoubted constitutional right of the people to meet freely, when, how, and where they choose, in public places, peaceably, in the day, to discuss their grievances and political or other subjects, or for the purpose of framing, discussing, or passing any vote, petition, or remonstrance, upon any subject whatsoever.

That your petitioners complain that the right has unconstitutionally been infringed, and 500 well disposed persons have been arrested, excessive bail demanded, tried by packed juries, sentenced to imprisonment, and treated as felons of the worst description.

That an unconstitutional police force is distributed all over the country, at enormous cost, to prevent the due exercise of the people's rights. And your petitioners are of opinion that the Poor-law Bastiles and the police stations, being co-existent, have originated from the same cause—viz., the increased desire on the part of the irresponsible few to oppress and starve the many.

That a vast and unconstitutional army is upheld at the public expense for the purpose of repressing public opinion in the three kingdoms, and likewise to intimidate the millions in the due exercise of those rights and privileges which ought to belong to them.

That your petitioners complain that the hours of labour, particularly of the factory workers, are protracted beyond the limits of human endurance, and that the wages earned, after unnatural application to toil in heated and unhealthy workshops, are inadequate to sustain the bodily strength and supply those comforts which are so imperative after an excessive waste of physical energy.

That your petitioners also direct the attention of your honourable House to the starvation wages of the agricultural labourer, and view with horror and indignation the paltry income of those whose toil gives being to the staple food of this people.

That your petitioners deeply deplore the existence of any kind of monopoly in this nation, and whilst they unequivocally condemn the levying of any tax upon the necessaries of life, and upon those articles principally required by the labouring classes, they are also sensible that the abolition of any one monopoly will never unshackle labour from its misery until the people possess that power under which all monopoly and oppression must cease; and your petitioners respectfully mention the existing monopolies of the suffrage, of paper money, of machinery, of land, of the public press, of religious privileges, of the means of travelling and transit, and a host of other evils too numerous to mention, all arising from class legislation, but which your honourable House has always consistently endeavoured to increase instead of diminish.

That your petitioners are sensible, from the numerous petitions presented to your honourable House, that your honourable House is fully acquainted with the grievances of the working men; and your petitioners pray that the rights and wrongs of labour may be considered, with a view to the protection of the one, and to the removal of the other; because your petitioners are of the opinion that it is the worst species of legislation which leaves the grievances of society to be removed only by violence or revolution, both of which may be apprehended if complaints are unattended to and petitions despised.

That your petitioners complain that upwards of nine millions of pounds per annum are unjustly abstracted from them to maintain a Church establishment from which they principally dissent; and beg to call the attention of your honourable House to the fact that this enormous sum is equal to, if it does not exceed, the cost of upholding Christianity in all parts of the world beside. Your petitioners complain that it is unjust, and not in accordance with the Christian religion, to enforce compulsory support of religious creeds, and expensive Church establishments, with which the people do not agree.

*   *   *   *   *

That your petitioners, therefore, exercising their just constitutional right, demand that your honourable House do remedy the many gross and manifest evils of which your petitioners complain, do immediately, without alteration, deduction, or addition, pass into a law the document entitled, "The People's Charter," which embraces the representation of male adults, vote by ballot, annual Parliaments, no property qualification, payment of members, and equal electoral districts.

And that your petitioners, desiring to promote the peace of the United Kingdom, security of property, and prosperity of commerce, seriously and earnestly press this, their petition, on the attention of your honourable House.

And your petitioners, etc.

Petition to be printed.

THE RAILWAY BOOM (1842).

Endymion

Source.—Lord Beaconsfield's *Endymion*, bk. iii., chap. x.

The condition of England at the meeting of Parliament in 1842 was not satisfactory. The depression of trade in the manufacturing districts seemed overwhelming, and continued increasing during the whole of the year. A memorial from Stockport to the Queen in the spring represented that more than half the master-spinners had failed, and that no less than three thousand dwelling-houses were untenanted. One-fifth of the population of Leeds were dependent on the poor-rates. The state of Sheffield was not less severe—and the blast furnaces of Wolverhampton were extinguished. There were almost daily meetings at Liverpool, Manchester, and Leeds, to consider the great and increasing distress of the country, and to induce ministers to bring forward remedial measures; but as these were impossible, violence was soon substituted for passionate appeals to the fears or the humanity of the Government. Vast bodies of the population assembled in Stalybridge, and Ashton, and Oldham, and marched into Manchester.

For a week the rioting was unchecked, but the Government despatched a strong military force to that city, and order was restored.

The state of affairs in Scotland was not more favourable. There were food riots in several of the Scotch towns, and in Glasgow the multitude assembled, and then commenced what they called a begging tour, but which was really a progress of not disguised intimidation. The economic crisis in Ireland was yet to come, but the whole of that country was absorbed in a harassing and dangerous agitation for the repeal of the union between the two countries.

During all this time, the Anti-Corn-Law League was holding regular and frequent meetings at Manchester, at which statements were made, distinguished by much eloquence and little scruple. But the able leaders of this confederacy never succeeded in enlisting the sympathies of the great body of the population. Between the masters and the workmen there was an alienation of feeling, which apparently never could be removed. This reserve, however, did not enlist the working classes on the side of the Government; they had their own object, and one which they themselves enthusiastically cherished. And this was the Charter, a political settlement which was to restore the golden age, and which the master manufacturers and the middle classes generally looked upon with even more apprehension than Her Majesty's advisers. It is hardly necessary to add, that in a state of affairs like that which is here faintly but still faithfully sketched, the rapid diminution of the revenue was inevitable, and of course that decline mainly occurred in the two all-important branches of the customs and excise....

The minister brought forward his revision of the tariff, which was denounced by the League as futile, and in which anathema the opposition soon found it convenient to agree. Had the minister included in his measure that "total and immediate repeal" of the existing corn laws which was preached by many as a panacea, the effect would have been probably much the same. No doubt a tariff may aggravate, or may mitigate, such a condition of commercial depression as periodically visits a state of society like that of England, but it does not produce it. It was produced in 1842, as it has been produced at the present time,[1] by an abuse of capital and credit, and by a degree of production which the wants of the world have not warranted.

And yet all this time, there were certain influences at work in the great body of the nation, neither foreseen, nor for some time recognised, by statesmen and those great capitalists on whose opinion statesmen much depend, which were stirring, as it were, like the unconscious power of the forces of nature, and which were destined to baffle all the calculations of persons in authority and the leading spirits of all parties, strengthen a perplexed administration, confound a sanguine opposition, render all the rhetoric, statistics, and subscriptions of the Anti-Corn-Law fruitless, and absolutely make the Chartists forget the Charter.

There was abundant capital in the country and a mass of unemployed labour. But the markets on which they had of late depended, the American especially, were overworked and overstocked, and in some instances were not only overstocked, but disturbed by war, as the Chinese, for example—and capital and labour wanted a new channel.

The new channel came, and all the persons of authority, alike political and commercial, seemed quite surprised that it had arrived; but when a thing or a man is wanted, they generally appear. One or two lines of railway which had been long sleepily in formation, about this time were finished, and one or two lines of railway which had been finished for some time and were unnoticed, announced dividends, and not contemptible ones. Suddenly there was a general feeling in the country that its capital should be invested in railways; that the whole surface of the land should be transformed, and covered, as by a network, with these mighty means of communication. When the passions of the English, naturally an enthusiastic people, are excited on a subject of finance, their will, their determination, and resource, are irresistible. This was signally proved in the present instance, for they never ceased subscribing their capital until the sum entrusted to this new form of investment reached an amount almost equal to the national debt; and this, too, in a very few years. The immediate effect on the condition of the country was absolutely prodigious. The value of land rose, all the blast furnaces were relit, a stimulant was given to every branch of the home trade, the amount suddenly paid in wages exceeded that ever known in this country, and wages, too, at a high rate. Large portions of the labouring classes not only enjoyed comfort, but commanded luxury. All this of course soon acted on the revenue, and both customs and espe-

[1] *Endymion* was published in 1880.

cially excise soon furnished an ample surplus.

It cannot be pretended that all this energy and enterprise were free in their operation from those evils which, it seems, must inevitably attend any extensive public speculation, however well-founded. Many of the scenes and circumstances recalled the days of the South Sea Scheme. The gambling in shares of companies which were formed only in name was without limit. The principal towns of the north established for that purpose stock exchanges of their own, and Leeds especially, one-fifth of whose population had been authoritatively described in the first session of the new parliament as dependent on the poor-rates, now boasted of a stock exchange which in the extent of its transactions rivalled that of the metropolis. And the gambling was universal, from the noble to the mechanic. It was confined to no class and no sex. The scene which took place at the Board of Trade on the last day on which plans could be lodged, and when midnight had arrived while crowds from the country were still filling the hall, and pressing at the doors, deserved and required for its adequate representation the genius of a Hogarth. This was the day on which it was announced that the total number of railway projects, on which deposits had been paid, had reached nearly to eight hundred.

What is remarkable in this vast movement in which so many millions were produced, and so many more promised, is, that the great leaders of the financial world took no part in it. The mighty loan-mongers on whose fiat the fate of kings and empires sometimes depended, seemed like men who, witnessing some eccentricity of nature, watch it with mixed feelings of curiosity and alarm. Even Lombard Street, which never was more wanted, was inactive, and it was only by the irresistible pressure of circumstances that a banking firm which had an extensive country connection was ultimately forced to take the leading part that was required, and almost unconsciously lay the foundation of the vast fortunes which it has realised, and organise the varied connection which it now commands. All seemed to come from the provinces, and from unknown people in the provinces.

THE CORN LAWS
AND THE MANUFACTURERS (1842).

Hansard

Source.—*Hansard*, Third Series, vol. 60, col. 420.

[NOTE.—The speech from which the following extracts are made was delivered in the House of Commons on February 14, 1842, on Sir R. Peel's Motion for the House to go into Committee on his proposed sliding scale of Corn Duties.]

MR. FERRAND: Sir, during the recess I thought it my duty to watch the proceedings of the Anti-Corn-Law League, who were agitating the country by the most violent and infamous placards, headed in large letters—"the base, bloody, and brutal landlords keep the bread of life from the poor"; and who were sending forth agitators, uttering falsehoods even more horrible than this, to pay whose expenses they have lately been exposing their wives and daughters at Manchester to the insolence of every coxcomb who chose to pay a shilling for his amusement. I also made inquiries into the truth of their assertions that the Corn Laws were the cause of the depression of trade, and of the misery and starvation of the working classes; and I found that during the operation of the Corn Laws in the last twenty years the Messrs. Marshall, flax-spinners of Leeds, have accumulated two millions in money, and have purchased immense landed estates; but this firm were not satisfied with this enormous wealth; they must carry out by themselves the principle of free trade, and set up mills in Belgium, where there are no Corn Laws, and where labour is at a starvation price.... I will add a few more instances of the injurious effects of the Corn Laws on Anti-Corn-Law League manufacturers. I am credibly informed that the credit of the hon. Member for Manchester (Mr. M. Philips) stands as high as ever on the Exchange in Manchester—that he is still a man of immense wealth, and has purchased extensive landed estates. The hon. Member for Stockport (Mr. Cobden) had during these last twelve years accumulated half-a-million of money, and when, night after night during the last Session, he was asserting that the Corn Laws had ruined the trade in Lancashire, he was actually, at that very time, running his mill both day and night; but, Sir, I must admit that the hon. Member for Bolton (Dr. Bowring) has produced the only argument in favour of a repeal of the Corn Laws; for his opposition to them has enabled him to practise his principles of free trade on the public purse to such an extent as very fairly to have entitled him to the character of a freebooter.

Sir, these Anti-Corn-Law agitators assert that great numbers of the manufacturers in the country are insolvent, and that the Corn Laws are the cause of that insolvency. Sir, I have inquired into the truth of this assertion, and I am sorry to say that as far as the insolvency goes, it is but too correct. The Corn Laws, however, are not the cause; the reason is—these men were never solvent in their lives. I will now, Sir, endeavour to explain to the House who are the manufacturers in the north of England in the present day. They are a remnant of that high-minded and honourable class of men who raised the trade of this country to the highest pitch of commercial respectability. There are a few, Sir, who still endeavour to tread in the steps of these men; but they have to contend against men who are gambling speculators in trade, and who know no bounds to their insatiate thirst for wealth, a body of men trading with false capital under the shelter of Joint Stock Banks, many of which are themselves little better than societies formed for the protection of swindling. These men get their names entered in the books of one of these banks, they then wait upon a woolstapler, and offer to purchase a quantity of wool, making use of this Joint Stock Bank as a reference for character and capital—the reply, of course, is, "Oh, they are highly respectable—they have their accounts in our books—you are quite safe." They then purchase the wool at three months' credit, have it converted by their power mills into goods, and dispose of it at market during the ensuing week for ready money. The consequence is, that they have to sacrifice a large amount, not only to the merchant, but also to the woolstapler, who is not paid in cash at the end of the three months, but in two months' bills. These men go on very prosperously so long as there is a brisk demand for the goods in the market, but when there is a stagnation in trade, caused by their recklessly overglutting the market, they inevitably become bankrupts.... I will now, Sir, inform the House what are the ultimate designs of this Anti-Corn-Law League. They commenced their operations three years ago. At first they only attempted an alteration of the Corn Laws; but finding very few supporters in the country, they held out a promise to the enemies of the Established Church, that if they would assist them in obtaining a total repeal of those laws, they would then join them in an attack upon that Establishment; a treaty being ratified between these parties, the hon. Member for Cork (Mr. O'Connell) was immediately invited over to take a seat at their first banquet. They there declared that the League was possessed of sufficient capital "to buy up" the landed property of the whole English nobility. But, Sir, I would ask what have the farmers to expect from these cotton lords when they have bought up the landed property of the country? It is their practice when they purchase land to have it immediately re-valued. They carry the principle of the ledger into their rent-roll; the rents are doubled; and I have known many families in my part of the country ruined by the oppression of these men. The manufacturing members of this League also want to increase their profits by reducing the price of wages; they also want to become the corn merchants of England; to convert one floor of their mills into a granary, and employ part of their machinery to grind the corn. [*Laughter.*] Hon. Members may laugh, but you cannot deceive the working classes; you have tried to make them believe differently; but all your hired agitators have failed to do so. Yes, the poor of England would have to go down to these men in the manufacturing districts with money in their sacks' mouths to buy corn, for there would be a great famine in the land. But this was only a part of their designs; now mark what would follow. Have hon. Members never been told of the Truck System? Have they never heard of the labourers' wages being paid in goods? Lest they should not, I will expose to the House such a system of tyranny, oppression, and plunder, committed on these half-starved operatives, as is a disgrace to any Christian country. Sir, when the poor labourers go to receive their work from these manufacturers they now find that it generally consists of a very inferior article. They find the wool difficult to comb, and the warps full of flaws. On the Saturday evening—that period which ought to be the sweetest hour of the week to the working man—when the reward of his labour ought to be as freely given as it would ever be gratefully received—even this is pilfered from him. He takes his work to the mill, and who do you think receives it? Not the master of the mill—no, but an overlooker, who pretends carefully to examine it, and, of course, finds fault with it. He says to the poor fellow, "You have done this work ill; I must deduct so much from your combing." And the poor weavers, who are perhaps only receiving three and sixpence or four shillings a week, are constantly mulcted in this manner by these overlookers, who have their own wages paid out of what they can deduct from these plundered wretches, and a percentage on the amount. Then, again, mark what follows: they have not even the small remnant paid in money; it is paid in goods, in rotten corn, in "cheap flour"; and when the poor man carries it home to his wife and family, after in vain endeavouring to induce the master to pay him his wages in money, he finds the flour which he had received as wages in the previous week still unconsumed, the quality being so bad that the stomachs of his sickly children had been unable to retain it. Sir, I assert that all this is true, for I have heard these statements during the course of my life from hundreds of the working classes; and what is more, they say that they have no hope of relief or succour from the Anti-Corn-Law League. Sir, these manufacturers are the men for whom the landed interest of England is to be destroyed!—these are the men for whom the yeomanry of Great Britain are to be driven from their homes!—these are the men who are to become the possessors of the English soil!—men who live and move and have their being for money alone; they care not how they obtain it; what cruelty and oppression they inflict, so long as they amass wealth from the sweat of the poor man's brow. They refuse him the price of his labour; they look for nothing but enormous profits; they declare that there is no religion in trade; in short, they are, to use the emphatic language of Mr. Burke, a set of men whose ledger is their bible, whose counting-house is their church, and whose money is their God!

IMPRISONMENT FOR ABSENCE FROM CHURCH (1842)

Hansard

Source.—*Hansard*, Third Series, vol. 60, col. 309.

Mr. Monckton Milnes said, it might be in the recollection of some Members of that House, that towards the end of last Session he gave notice of his intention to move for leave to bring in a Bill for the repeal of so much of certain acts of Elizabeth and James I. as inflicted penalties for the non-attendance on divine worship. The circumstances to which his motion applied would be found stated in the sixth report of the Inspectors of Prisons, published last year; the case had attracted great attention, and the vigilant eye of the press, to which public justice owed so much, had been directed to it in such a manner as to render it impossible that the case should not come before Parliament in some way or other. He thought, therefore, that it was better that the case should be brought under the notice of the House by one who, as far as he is known at all, is known as a humble and attached member of the Church of England rather than by any one indifferent or even hostile to that sacred institution. The cases to which he particularly wished to advert were stated in page 79 of the report, and are described by the Inspector as follows:

> "Among other complaints made to me by prisoners, J. C. came forward and stated that he was placed in the Ecclesiastical Court, and sentenced to pay a fine of one shilling and fourteen shillings costs; that he had been in prison ten weeks, and had no means of paying, and hoped that a representation might be made of his case, or he must remain a prisoner for ever. Upon referring to this man's commitment, I find that he was summarily convicted before two magistrates, that on the _______ June, being the Lord's Day, called Sunday, in the township of _______, did neglect to attend a church, or at some other place of religious worship, on the said day, he not having any reasonable excuse to be absent, and adjudged to forfeit and pay one shilling together with fourteen shillings costs, and in default to be kept in prison until the said sums shall be paid. It appeared that the following number of persons had been committed for a similar offence, and been discharged upon payment of the fine and costs:

Name.	When received in Prison.	Fine.		Costs.			Period of Confinement.
	1839.	s.	d.	£	s.	d.	
J. B.	February 12	1	0	0	10	6	63 days
J. S.	February 12	1	0	0	10	6	61 days
W. W.	April 15	1	0	0	19	0	16 days
J. S.	April 22	1	0	0	13	0	12 days
G. B.	August 5	1	0	1	4	0	17 days
J. K.	August 6	1	0	0	11	0	2 days
A. G.	November 4	1	0	0	17	6	16 days
B. K.	November 6	1	0	0	7	0	26 days
P. F.	December 13	1	0	0	12	6	3 days
T. R.	December 23	1	0	0	16	0	27 days
	1840.						
T. S.	May 10	1	0	0	12	0	3 days

The poverty of the prisoner J. C. appearing to be such as to leave no hope of his being able to pay the fine and costs, I decided on making a representation of his case to the Secretary of State, who was pleased to recommend him forthwith as a fitting object for her Majesty's pardon, and he was discharged in consequence.

He (Mr. Monckton Milnes) believed that in all those cases the parties proceeded against were simple labouring men, who would have been totally incapable of paying the fines inflicted upon them, if the case had not attracted the notice of her Majesty's Ministers; and it may be remarked, that in the first case the man was kept in prison during the whole hay-time and harvest, and was thus prevented from earning the means of his winter sustenance.... In a question of abuse of this nature, it was but natural that they should enquire what was the conduct of the magistrates. He had communicated with one of these magistrates, who had written:

A man is brought before the magistrates charged with drunkenness in its most offensive form on the Sabbath, and with neglecting church. On enquiry it is found that this is his habitual practice, and that his conduct in this state renders him a pest to the neighbourhood. Perhaps even you will admit that such a character deserves punishment, and that he ought to be fined for drunkenness. Well, fine him. He refuses to pay, and has no goods on which to distrain. What then is to be done? Put him in the stocks, the law says; but we have no stocks, and the vagabond escapes scot free. To prevent this result and in respect to such characters only, recourse has been had to the statute enabling magistrates to fine for non-attendance at public worship, under which committals follow in case of non-payment."

A CHARTIST IN PRISON (1843).

Life of Thomas Cooper

Source.—*The Life of Thomas Cooper*, written by himself, p. 237. (London: 1872.)

[NOTE.—Thomas Cooper was convicted in 1843 of sedition in connection with a riot at Hanley, and sentenced to two years' imprisonment.]

Each cell had a stone floor; was simply long enough to hold a bed, and broad enough for one to walk by the side of it. An immense slab of cast-iron formed the bedstead, and it rested on two large stones. A bag stuffed so hard with straw that you could scarcely make an impression on it with your heel, formed the bed. Two blankets and a rug completed the furniture. There was no pillow; but remembering that from my former imprisonment, I had brought in with me a small macintosh pillow which I could blow up and put under my head. The best thing I had was a very large and very heavy camlet travelling cloak. If I had not brought this with me, I could not have slept in that cell during the winter without becoming a cripple for life, or losing my life.

The prison bell rang at half-past five, and we were expected to rise and be ready to descend into the day-yard at six. At eight, they brought us a brown porringer, full of "skilly"—for it was such bad unpalatable oatmeal gruel that it deserved the name—and a loaf of coarse, dark-coloured bread. At twelve at noon, they unlocked the door of our day-room, and threw upon the deal table a netful of boiled potatoes, in their skins, and a paper of salt—for dinner. At five in the evening they brought us half a porringer of "skilly," but no bread. At six, we were trooped off, and locked up in our sleeping cells for the next twelve hours.

I demanded better food; and was told I could not have it. I asked to write to my wife, and receive a letter from her; but still they refused. One day I slipped past one of the turnkeys as he unlocked our day-room door, ran along the passages, and got to the governor's room, and thundered at it till he came out in alarm.

"Give me food that I can eat," I said, "or some of you shall pay for it."

"Go back—get away to your day-room," cried the governor.

"I will, if you will give me something to eat," I said.

"Here—come here and take him away!" cried the governor to two of the turnkeys who had just then appeared, but who looked sorely affrighted.

"I'll knock the first man down who dares to touch me," said I; and the turnkeys stood still.

The governor burst into laughter, for he saw they were plainly in a fix.

"What d'ye want to eat, Cooper?" said he in a gentle tone; "tell me, and I'll give it you."

"All I want of you at present," said I, "is a cup of good coffee, and a hearty slice of bread and butter. When I can speak to the magistrates, I shall ask for something more."

And I did ask the magistrates; but they would not yield. So I led the officers of the prison a sorely harassing life—poor fellows! I was ever knocking at the door, or shattering the windows, or asking for the surgeon or governor, or troubling them in one way or other.

A CHARTIST HYMN (1843).

Life of Thomas Cooper

Source.—*The Life of Thomas Cooper*, written by himself. (London: 1872.)

Sons of poverty assemble,
Ye whose hearts with woe are riven,
Let the guilty tyrants tremble,
Who your hearts such pain have given.
We will never
From the shrine of truth be driven.

Must ye faint—ah! how much longer?
Better by the sword to die
Than to die of want and hunger:
They heed not your feeble cry:
Lift your voices—
Lift your voices to the sky.

Rouse them from their silken slumbers,
Trouble them amidst their pride:
Swell your ranks, augment your numbers,
Spread the Charter far and wide!
Truth is with us:
God Himself is on our side.

See the brave, ye spirit-broken,
That uphold your righteous cause;
Who against them hath not spoken?
They are, just as Jesus was,
Persecuted
By bad men and wicked laws.

Dire oppression, Heaven decrees it,
From our land shall soon be hurled:
Mark the coming time and seize it—
Every banner be unfurled!
Spread the Charter!
Spread the Charter through the world.

FORETASTES OF DARWINISM (1844).

Tancred

Source. — Lord Beaconsfield's *Tancred*, bk. ii., chap. ix.

Lady Constance took up a book which was at hand, and said: "Do you know this?" And Tancred, opening a volume which he had never seen, found it was "The Revelations of Chaos" — a startling work just published, and of which a rumour had reached him.

"No," he replied, "I have not seen it."

"I will lend it you if you like; it is one of those books one must read. It explains everything, and is written in a very agreeable style."

"It explains everything!" said Tancred. "It must indeed be a very remarkable book."

"I think it will just suit you," said Lady Constance. "Do you know, I thought so several times while I was reading it."

"To judge from the title, the subject is rather obscure," said Tancred.

"No longer so," said Lady Constance. "It is treated scientifically; everything is explained by geology and astronomy, and in that way. It shows you exactly how a star is formed; nothing can be so pretty! A cluster of vapour — the cream of the Milky Way — a sort of celestial cheese — churned into light. You must read it; 'tis charming."

"Nobody ever saw a star formed," said Tancred.

"Perhaps not. You must read the 'Revelations'; it is all explained. But what is most interesting is the way in which man has been developed. You know, all is development. The principle is perpetually going on. First there was nothing, then there was something, then — I forget the next; I think there were shells, then fishes, then we came. Let me see — did we come next? Never mind that; we came at last. And the next change there will be something very superior to us — something with wings. Ah! that's it. We were fishes, and I believe we shall be crows. But you must read it."

"I do not believe I ever was a fish," said Tancred.

"Oh, but it is all proved! You must not argue on my rapid sketch; read the book. It is impossible to contradict anything in it. You understand, it is all science; it is not like those books in which one says one thing and another the contrary, and both may be wrong. Everything is proved—by geology, you know. You see exactly how everything is made; how many worlds there have been; how long they lasted; what went before; what comes next. We are a link in the chain, as inferior animals were that preceded us. We in turn shall be inferior; all that will remain of us will be some relics in a new red sandstone. This is development. We had fins; we may have wings."

THE OPENING OF MAZZINI'S LETTERS (1844).

Hansard

Source.—*Hansard*, Third Series, vol. 76, col. 212.

[NOTE.—On June 14, 1844, Mr. Duncombe, the friend of the Chartists, presented in the House of Commons a petition by W. J. Linton, Joseph Mazzini, and others, complaining that their letters had been opened at the General Post Office, and urging that such a practice, introducing as it did the spy system of foreign states, was repugnant to every principle of the British Constitution, and subversive of the public confidence. A debate followed on July 2, when Mr. Duncombe moved for a Committee of Inquiry.]

Mr. Thomas Duncombe said he did not retract one single charge that he had made—viz., that within the last two years there had been a most unscrupulous use made of the power vested in the Government in opening the letters of different parties, and to a very great extent; and he believed that if an inquiry were instituted, he should be able to prove that so far from the Right Hon. Baronet (Sir James Graham, the Home Secretary) having only done what every Secretary of State had done since the time of Queen Anne, there had been more letters opened contrary to law within the last two years than had been opened within the last ten or twenty years. He understood that there existed in the General Post Office an office which was commonly called or known by the subordinates of the establishments, as well as by the superior officers, as "the secret or Inner Office." In this office these deeds of darkness took place. It was a sort of Star Chamber—a sort of Post Office Inquisition. Letters were carried into that place, where they were examined, and from thence a message was sent to the Home Office, and copies were taken of these letters, according to the value of their contents.... He understood, and that was capable of contradiction if not true, that at this moment day after day the letters of Foreign Ministers were opened and read; that at all events they went into some other office, and no one could tell whether they had been opened or not.... It was said before that it was an un-English custom, but it now appeared to be peculiarly English, particularly in the way we carried it out; for he found that in Austria even, if not always, but nine times out of ten, whenever any letters were opened they were re-sealed with the government seal, by which it was known that they had been opened by authority. And very often Ferdinand, Grand Duke of Tuscany, after perusing letters detained at the Post Office, was in the habit of writing underneath, "Vidit Ferdinandus." In England there had never been an instance of any mark being made of a letter having been secretly read at the Post Office, but on all occasions the party was kept in ignorance of his secrets having been disclosed to the Government.... They had opened letters at the instigation of Foreign Powers, and to a very great extent—the letters of Polish exiles, Italians, and others. What had this been done for? What had we to do with misunderstandings in Italy? How little was it known by foreigners that England was guilty of such treachery. Mazzini himself, only the other day, received a letter from one of his expatriated countrymen, who had taken refuge at Corfu, dated May 1, who wrote thus—perhaps the right hon. Baronet had seen this letter: "Now that I have got my foot on British soil, relying upon the well-known loyalty of Englishmen, you may write to me in my own name." Poor deluded man! What did he do in this letter besides? He thanked the individuals who had assisted him in his escape. These names were found in this letter, the letter was handed over to the Austrian Government, and these individuals were thrown into prison. At this moment fifty or sixty persons were in prison, suffering imprisonment because of the base information of the British to their ambassador, and communicated by the ambassador to his own Government.

AGRICULTURE AND FREE TRADE (1845).

Hansard

Source.—*Hansard*, Third Series, vol. 78, col. 785, March 13.

Mr. Cobden, having presented a petition in favour of his Motion for a Committee of Inquiry into the effects of the Corn Laws on Agriculturists, addressed the House: Sir, the object of this Motion is to appoint a Select Committee to inquire into the present condition of the agricultural interests; and at the same time to ascertain how the laws regulating the importation of agricultural produce have affected the agriculturists of this country. As regards the distress among farmers, I presume we cannot go to a higher authority than those hon. Gentlemen who profess to be the farmers' friends and protectors. I find it stated by those hon. Gentlemen who recently paid their respects to the Prime Minister, that the agriculturists are in a state of great embarrassment and distress. I find that one gentleman from Norfolk (Mr. Hudson) stated that the farmers in the county are paying their rents, but paying them out of capital, and not profits. I find that Mr. Turner, of Upton, in Devonshire, stated that one-half of the smaller farmers in that county are insolvent, and that the others are rapidly falling into the same condition; that the farmers with larger holdings are quitting their farms with a view of saving the rest of their property; and that, unless some remedial measures are adopted by this House, they will be utterly ruined. The accounts which I have given you of those districts are such as I have had from many other sources. I put it to county members, whether—taking the whole of the south of England, from the confines of Nottinghamshire to the Land's End—whether, as a rule, the farmers are not now in a state of the greatest embarrassment? ...

I am at a loss to understand what protection to agriculture means, because I find such contradictory accounts given in this House by the promoters of that system. For instance, nine months ago, when my right hon. friend the member for Wolverhampton (Mr. Villiers) brought forward his Motion for the Abolition of the Corn Laws, the right hon. gentleman, then the President of the Board of Trade, in replying to him, said that the present Corn Law had been most successful in its operations. He took great credit to the Government for the steadiness of price that was obtained under that law. Now recollect that the right hon. gentleman was speaking when wheat was 56s. a quarter, and that wheat is now 45s. The right hon. Baronet at the head of the Government says: "My legislation has had nothing to do with wheat being at 45s. a quarter"; but how are we to get over the difficulty that the responsible member of Government at the head of the Board of Trade, only nine months ago, claimed merit for the Government to have kept up the price of wheat at 56s.? These discrepancies themselves between members of the Government and its supporters render it more and more necessary that this question of protection should be inquired into. I ask, what does it mean? The price of wheat is 45s. this day. I have been speaking to the highest authority in England on this point—one who is often quoted by this House—within the last week, and he tells me that, with another favourable harvest, he thinks it very likely that wheat will be 35s. a quarter. What does this legislation mean, or what does it purport to be, if you are to have prices fluctuating from 56s. down to 35s. a quarter, and probably lower? Can you prevent it by the legislation of this House? ...

I show you after thirty years' trial what is the depressed condition of the agriculturists; I prove to you what is the impoverished state of farmers, and also of the labourers, and you will not contest any one of those propositions. I say it is enough, having had thirty years' trial of your specific with no better results than these, for me to ask you to go into Committee to see if something better cannot be devised. I am going to contend that free trade in grain would be more advantageous to farmers—and with them I include labourers—than restriction; to oblige the hon. member for Norfolk, I will take with them also the landlords; and I contend that free trade in corn and grain of every kind would be more beneficial to them than to any other class of the community. I should have contended the same before the passing of the late tariff. But now I am prepared to do so with tenfold more force. What has the right hon. Baronet (Sir R. Peel) done? He has passed a law to admit fat cattle at a nominal duty. Some foreign fat cattle were selling in Smithfield the other day at about £15 or £16 per head, paying only about 7-½ per cent. duty; but he has not admitted the raw material out of which these fat cattle are made. I say, give free trade in that grain which goes to make the cattle. I contend that by this protective system the farmers throughout the country are more injured than any other class in the community. I would take, for instance, the article of clover-seed. I believe clover-seed is to be excluded from the schedule of free importation. Now I ask for whose benefit is this exception made? I ask the hon. member for North Northamptonshire, whether those whom he represents, the farmers of that district, are, in a large majority of instances, sellers of clover-seed? I will undertake to say they are not. How many counties in England are there which are benefited by the protection of clover-seed? I will take the whole of Scotland. If there be any Scotch members present, I ask them whether they do not in their country import the clover-seed from England? They do not grow it. I undertake to say there are not ten counties in the United Kingdom which are interested in the exportation of clover-seed out of their own borders. Neither have they any of this article in Ireland. But yet we have clover-seed excluded from the farmers, although they are not interested as a body in its protection at all. Again, take the article of beans. There are lands in Essex where they can grow them alternate years with wheat. I find that beans come from that district to Mark Lane; and I believe also that in some parts of Lincolnshire and Cambridgeshire they do the same; but how is it with the poor lands of Surrey or the poor downland of Wiltshire? Take the whole of the counties. How many of them are there which are exporters of beans, or send them to market? You are taxing the whole of the farmers who do not sell their beans, for the pretended benefit of a few counties or districts of counties where they do. Mark you, where they can grow beans on the better and stronger soils, it is not in one case out of ten that they grow them for the market. They may grow them for their own use; but where they do not cultivate beans, send them to market, and turn them into money, those farmers can have no interest whatever in keeping up the money price of that which they never sell. Take the article of oats. How many farmers are there who ever have oats down on the credit side of their books, as an item upon which they rely for the payment of their rents? The farmers may, and generally do, grow oats for feeding their own horses; but it is an exception to the rule—and a rare exception, too—where the farmer depends upon the sale of his oats to meet his expenses. Take the article of hops. You have a protection upon them for the benefit of the growers in Kent, Sussex, and Surrey; but yet the cultivators of hops are taxed for the protection of others in articles which they do not themselves produce. Take the article of cheese. Not one farmer in ten in the country makes his own cheese, and yet they and their servants are large consumers of it. But what are the counties which have the protection in this article? Cheshire, Gloucestershire, Wiltshire, part of Derbyshire, and Leicestershire. Here are some four or five dairy counties having an interest in the protection of cheese; but recollect that those counties are peculiarly hardly taxed in beans and oats, because in those counties where they are chiefly dairy farms, they are most in want of artificial food for their cattle. There are the whole of the hilly districts; and I hope my friend the member for Nottingham (Mr. Gisborne) is here, because he has a special grievance in this matter; he lives in Derbyshire, and very commendably employs himself in rearing good cattle upon the hills; but he is taxed for your protection for his beans, peas, oats, Indian corn, and everything which he wants for feeding them. He told me, only the other day, that he should like nothing better than to give up the little remnant of protection on cattle, if you would only let him buy a thousand quarters of black oats for the consumption of his stock.... Take the whole of the hilly districts, and the down country of Wiltshire; the whole of that expanse of downs in the south of England; take the Cheviots, where the flockmasters reside; the Grampians in Scotland; and take the whole of Wales; they are not benefited in the slightest degree by the protection on these articles; but, on the contrary, you are taxing the very things they want. They require provender as abundantly and cheaply as they can get it. Allowing a free importation of food for cattle is the only way in which those counties can improve the breed of their lean stocks, and the only manner in which they can ever bring their land up to anything like a proper state of fertility. I will go further and say that farms with thin soil, which you will find in Hertfordshire and Surrey, farmers with large capital, arable farmers, I say those men are deeply interested in having a free importation of food for their cattle, because they have thin, poor land. The land does not of itself contain the means of increased fertility; and the only way is the bringing in of an additional quantity of food from elsewhere, that they can bring their farms up to a proper state of cultivation. I have been favoured with an estimate made by a very clever experienced farmer in Wiltshire. That gentleman estimates that upon every 400 acres of land he could increase his profits to the amount of £280, paying the same rent as at present, provided there was a free importation of foreign grain of all kinds. He would buy 500 quarters of oats at 15s., or the same amount in beans or peas at 14s. or 15s. a sack, to be fed on the land or in the yard; by which he would grow additional 160 quarters of wheat, and 230 quarters of barley, and gain an increased profit of £300 upon his sheep and cattle. His plan embraces the employment of an additional capital of £1,000; and he would pay £150 a year more for labour. I had an opportunity, the other day, of speaking to a very intelligent farmer in Hertfordshire. He told me that last year he paid £230 enhanced price on his beans and other provender which he bought for his cattle—£230 enhanced price in consequence of that restriction upon the trade in foreign grain, amounting to 14s. a quarter on all the wheat he sold off his farm.... I think I could give you from every county the names of some of the first-rate farmers who are as ardent free-traders as I am.... They say, "Let us have our Indian corn, Egyptian beans, and Polish oats, as freely as we have our linseed cake, and we can bear competition with any corn-growers in the world."

PEEL'S CHANGE OF VIEWS (1844).

Peel's Memoirs

Source.—*Memoirs by Sir Robert Peel*, vol. ii., p. 98. (London: 1858.)

I will briefly refer to the position of the Corn Law question at the close of the Session of 1845, unaffected as it then was by failure, or apprehension of failure, in any particular article of food.

The progress of discussion had made a material change in the opinions of many persons with regard to the policy of protection to domestic agriculture, and the extent to which this policy should be carried.

I had adopted at an early period of my public life, without, I fear, much serious reflection, the opinions generally prevalent at that time among men of all parties, as to the justice and necessity of protection to agriculture.

They were the opinions of Sir Henry Parnell and Mr. Ricardo, of Lord John Russell and Lord Melbourne, as well as of the Duke of Wellington, Mr. Canning, and Mr. Huskisson. I had, however, been a willing party, both in 1828 and 1842, to the reductions which took place in the amount of protection fixed by the Corn Law of 1815, a law which was based on the assumption that wheat could not profitably be grown at a price lower than eighty shillings a quarter.

One of the first acts of the Government over which I presided (the Government of August, 1841) was to propose a material change in the Corn Law of 1828.... That proposal was ultimately adopted, after considerable discussion in Cabinet, and a Bill was brought into the House of Commons at an early period of the Session of 1842, which finally passed into a law, providing for a material diminution in the amount of the import duties on the several kinds of foreign grain. The prohibition which then existed on the import of foreign cattle and meat was removed in the same Session, and their import permitted on moderate rates of duty. These changes, although they gave little satisfaction to the most eager opponents of the Corn Law, and were indeed denounced by some as perfectly nugatory, were not effected without great murmuring and some open opposition to the Government on the part of many of its supporters.

The Duke of Buckingham resigned his seat in the Cabinet rather than be a party to them, nor was it an easy matter to procure the unanimous adoption of the measures I proposed by the remaining members of the Government.

During the discussions in Parliament on the Corn Law of 1842 I was more than once pressed to give a guarantee (so far as a Minister could give it) that the amount of protection established by that law should be permanently adhered to; but, although I did not then contemplate the necessity for further change, I uniformly refused to fetter the discretion of the Government by any such assurances as those that were required from me. It is unnecessary for the purposes of this memoir that I should refer in detail to the events that took place between the passing of the Corn Bill in 1842 and the close of the Session in 1845. During that interval the opinions I had previously entertained on the subject of protection to agriculture had undergone a great change.

The main causes of that change are stated in a public letter which I addressed to my constituents shortly before the General Election of 1847, from which the following is an extract. The latter part of this extract refers to a question in some respects distinct—namely, the difficulty there would be in subsequently maintaining inviolate the Corn Law of 1842 in the event of its suspension in 1845 on account of apprehended scarcity. I will give, however, the extract entire, as the reasoning applies with nearly equal force to the principle of continued protection as well as to the policy of its revival after having been once in abeyance. The letter is dated July, 1847.

To the Electors of Tamworth.

My confidence in the validity of the reasons on which I had myself heretofore relied for the maintenance of restrictions on the import of corn had been materially weakened. It had been weakened by the conflict of arguments on the principle of a restrictive policy; by many concurring proofs that the wages of labour do not vary with the price of corn; by the contrast presented in two successive periods of dearth and abundance, in the health, morals, and tranquillity and general prosperity of the whole community; by serious doubts whether, in the present condition of this country, cheapness and plenty are not ensured for the future in a higher degree by the free intercourse in corn, than by restrictions on its importation for the purpose of giving protection to domestic agriculture.

It had been weakened also by the following considerations, which were in a great degree new elements in forming a judgment on this vital matter.

The general repeal of prohibitory duties, and the recent application of the principles of free trade to almost all articles of import from abroad, made the Corn Laws the object of more searching scrutiny and more invidious comment, and narrowed the ground on which their defence could be maintained.

Among the articles of foreign import prohibited up to the year 1842, and then admitted at low rates of duty, were some important articles of agricultural produce, salted and fresh meat, oxen, sheep, cows, etc. You probably recollect the panic which this admission caused—the forced sale of stock, the prophecies that it would be impossible to compete with the foreign grazier, and that meat would be reduced to threepence a pound. Five years have passed since this great change in the law took place, and your own experience will enable you to judge whether the panic was well founded, and whether the prophecies have been fulfilled.

The complete failure of these prophecies had naturally had its effect on public opinion with regard to the probable consequences of a free intercourse in other articles of agricultural produce.

There was another circumstance still more calculated to diminish apprehensions as to the risk of opening the corn market of this country to foreign competition. There has appeared of late years a tendency to increase in the consumption of articles of subsistence much more rapid than the increase in the population. It is difficult, if not impossible, on account of the absence of statistical information, to measure accurately that increase in the case of articles of first necessity, such as corn and meat; but it may be inferred from the relative consumption at different periods of articles in respect to which the comparison can be instituted.

The following is an account of some of the principal articles entered for home consumption in the years 1841 and 1846 respectively:

Articles.	1841.	1846.
Cocoa	1,930,764 lbs.	2,962,327 lbs.
Coffee	28,420,980 lbs.	36,781,391 lbs.
Currants	190,071 cwts.	359,315 cwts.
Rice	245,887 cwts.	466,961 cwts.
Pepper	2,750,790 lbs.	3,297,431 lbs.
Sugar	4,065,971 cwts.	5,231,845 cwts.
Molasses	402,422 cwts.	582,665 cwts.
Tea	36,681,877 lbs.	46,728,208 lbs.
Tobacco and Snuff	22,308,385 lbs.	27,001,908 lbs.
Brandy	1,165,137 gallons	1,515,954 gallons
Geneva	15,404 gallons	40,211 gallons
British Spirits	20,642,333 gallons	23,122,581 gallons
Malt, charged with duty	36,164,448 bushels	41,979,000 bushels

Surely it is impossible to refer to this comparative table without being forcibly struck by the rapid increase in the consumption of the articles which it embraces. Can there be a doubt that if the consumption of articles of a secondary necessity has been thus advancing, the consumption of articles of first necessity—of meat and of bread, for instance—has been making at least an equally rapid progress?

During the greater part of the period included in the return, from the middle of 1842 to the end of 1846, the free trade measures have been in operation. They have been in operation, therefore—concurrently, at least—with these evidences of the increasing ease and comfort of the people. Other causes have no doubt contributed to that ease and comfort; but even if the whole effect be assigned to those other causes—to railway enterprise or anything else—it does not affect my present argument. If there be from any cause a tendency to the consumption of articles of the first necessity much more rapid than the increase of population, the responsibility of undertaking to regulate the supply of food by legislative restraints, and the difficulty of maintaining these restraints in the event of any sudden check to prosperity or increased price of subsistence, will be greatly augmented; while, on the other hand, the danger to be apprehended from foreign competition is materially lessened.

It was from the combined influence of these various considerations—from diminished confidence in the necessity or advantage of protection; from the increasing difficulty of resisting the application to articles of food of those principles which had been gradually applied to so many other articles; from the result of the experiment made with regard to cattle and meat in 1842; from the evidences of rapidly increasing consumption; from the aggravation of every other difficulty in the maintenance of the Corn Laws by the fact of their suspension on the first real pressure—it was from the combined influence of such considerations that I came to the conclusion that the attempt to maintain those laws inviolate after their suspension would be impolitic, that the struggle for their maintenance would assume a new character, and that no advantage to be gained by success could counterbalance the consequences of failure, or even the evils attending protracted conflict.

Between the maintenance of the Corn Laws inviolate and a measure involving their ultimate repeal, I saw no middle course satisfactory or advantageous to any interest; I saw still less of satisfaction or advantage in indecision and irrational delay. I could not admit the incompetency of the present Parliament to deal with this as with every other question of public concern. There appeared to me, upon the whole, much less of public evil in the resolution finally to adjust the question of the Corn Laws than in any other that could be then adopted; and that being my deliberate conviction, I felt it to be my duty to incur the painful sacrifices which the acting upon that conviction must inevitably entail.

LORD J. RUSSELL QUICKENS THE PACE (1845).

Peel's Memoirs

Source.—*Memoirs by Sir R. Peel*, vol. ii., p. 175. (London: 1858.)

To the Electors of the City of London.

Gentlemen,

The present state of the country in regard to its supply of food cannot be viewed without apprehension. Forethought and bold precaution may avert any serious evils—indecision and procrastination may produce a state of suffering which it is frightful to contemplate.

Three weeks ago it was generally expected that Parliament would be immediately called together. The announcement that Ministers were prepared at that time to advise the Crown to summon Parliament, and to propose on their first meeting a suspension of the import duties on corn, would have caused orders at once to be sent to various parts of Europe and America for the purchase and transmission of grain for the consumption of the United Kingdom. An Order in Council dispensing with the law was neither necessary nor desirable. No party in Parliament would have made itself responsible for the destruction of a measure so urgent and so beneficial.

The Queen's Ministers have met and separated without affording us any promise of such seasonable relief.

It becomes us, therefore, the Queen's subjects, to consider how we can best avert, or at all events mitigate, calamities of no ordinary magnitude.

Two evils require your consideration. One of these is the disease in the potatoes, affecting very seriously parts of England and Scotland, and committing fearful ravages in Ireland.

The extent of this evil has not yet been ascertained, and every week, indeed, tends either to reveal unexpected disease, or to abate in some districts the alarm previously entertained. But there is one misfortune peculiar to the failure in this particular crop. The effect of a bad corn-harvest is, in the first place, to diminish the supply in the market and to raise the price—hence diminished consumption, and the privation of incipient scarcity, by which the whole stock is more equally distributed over the year, and the ultimate pressure is greatly mitigated; but the fear of the breaking out of this unknown disease in the potatoes induces the holders to hurry into the market, and thus we have at one and the same time rapid consumption and impending deficiency—scarcity of the article and cheapness of price. The ultimate suffering must thereby be rendered far more severe than it otherwise would be. The evil to which I have adverted may be owing to an adverse season, to a mysterious disease in the potato, to want of science or of care in propagating the plant. In any of these cases, Government is no more subject to blame for the failure of the potato crop than it was entitled to credit for the plentiful corn-harvests which we have lately enjoyed.

Another evil, however, under which we are suffering, is the fruit of Ministerial counsel and Parliamentary law. It is the direct consequence of an Act of Parliament passed three years ago, on the recommendation of the present advisers of the Crown. By this law, grain of all kinds has been made subject to very high duties on importation. These duties are so contrived that the worse the quality of the corn, the higher is the duty; so that when good wheat rises to 70s. a quarter, the average price of all wheat is 57s. or 58s. and the duty 15s. or 14s. a quarter. Thus the corn barometer points to fair, while the ship is bending under a storm.

This defect was pointed out many years ago by writers on the Corn Laws, and was urged upon the attention of the House of Commons when the present Act was under consideration.

But I confess that on the general subject, my views have in the course of twenty years undergone a great alteration. I used to be of opinion that corn was an exception to the general rules of political economy; but observation and experience have convinced me that we ought to abstain from all interference with the supply of food. Neither a Government nor a Legislature can ever regulate the corn market with the beneficial effects which the entire freedom of sale and purchase are sure of themselves to produce....

Let us, then, unite to put an end to a system which has been proved to be the blight of commerce, the bane of agriculture, the source of bitter divisions among classes, the cause of penury, fever, mortality and crime among the people.

But if this end is to be achieved, it must be gained by the unequivocal expression of the public voice. It is not to be denied that many elections for cities and towns in 1841, and some in 1845, appear to favour the assertion that free-trade is not popular with the great mass of the community. The Government appear to be waiting for some excuse to give up the present Corn Law. Let the people by petition, by address, by remonstrance, afford them the excuse they seek. Let the Ministry propose such a revision of the taxes as in their opinion may render the public burdens more just and more equal; let them add any other provisions which caution and even scrupulous forbearance may suggest; but let the removal of restrictions on the admission of the main articles of food and clothing used by the mass of the people be required, in plain terms, as useful to all great interests, and indispensable to the progress of the nation.

J. RUSSELL.

EDINBURGH,
November 22, 1845.

THE BOMBSHELL (1845).

Greville Memoirs

Source. — *The Greville Memoirs*: 1837-1852, vol. ii., p. 309.

LONDON, *December 5.* — I came to town yesterday, and find public affairs in a state of the greatest interest and excitement. The whole town had been electrified in the morning by an article in the *Times* announcing with an air of certainty and authority that the discussions and disputes in the Cabinet had terminated by a resolution to call Parliament together early in January and propose a total repeal of the Corn Laws, and that the Duke had not only consented, but was to bring forward the measure in the House of Lords.... There can be very little doubt that it was Aberdeen's object that Delane should publish what he did, although he did not tell him to do so, and the reason is very obvious. Yesterday the American mail went off, and took with it the morning papers, and consequently this article in the *Times*. It was exactly what Aberdeen wanted. As Foreign Secretary, his most earnest desire is to get over the Oregon affair as well as he can, and he knows that nothing will have so great an effect in America, nothing tend so materially to the prevalence of pacific counsels, as an announcement that our Corn Laws are going to be repealed.

PEEL AND HIS COLLEAGUES (1845).

Queen Victoria's Letters

Source.—*Letters of Queen Victoria*: 1837-1861, vol. ii., p. 56. (London: 1907.)

Memorandum by the Prince Albert.

Osborne,
December 7th, 1845.

Yesterday, Sir Robert Peel arrived here, and explained the condition of affairs.... Sir Robert proposed, by opening the ports, a preparation for the abolition of the Corn Laws. His colleagues refused, and of the whole Cabinet only Lord Aberdeen, Sir James Graham, and Mr. Sidney Herbert voted with him. Sir Robert hoped that in time the opinions of others would change, and therefore postponed a final decision. In the meanwhile the agitation of the Anti-Corn-Law League began; in every town addresses were voted, meetings were held, the *Times*—barometer of public feeling—became violently Anti-Corn-Law, the meetings of the Cabinet roused attention, a general panic seized on the mass of the public....

When he (Sir Robert Peel) arrived here, he was visibly much moved....

On my observing that Sir Robert has a majority of one hundred in the House of Commons, and asking whether it was not possible for him to continue the Government, he said:

"The Duke of Buccleuch will carry half Scotland with him, and Lord Stanley, leading the Protectionists in the House of Lords, would lead to great and immediate defections even in Her Majesty's household. The Duchess of Buccleuch, Lord Hardwicke, Lord Exeter, Lord Rivers, Lord Beverley, etc., would resign, and we should not be able to find successors; in the House of Commons I am sure I should be beat, the Tories, agriculturists, etc., in rage would turn round upon me and be joined by the Whigs and Radicals, who would say: 'This is *our* measure, and we will not allow you to carry it.' It is better that I should go now, when *nobody has committed himself* in the heat of party contest, when no factions have been formed, no imprudent declarations made."

After we had examined what possibilities were open for the Crown, the conclusion was come to that Lord John was the only man who could be charged with forming a Cabinet. Lord Stanley, with the aristocracy as his base, would bring about an insurrection (or riots), and the ground on which one would have to fight would be this: to want to force the masses of the people, amid the great poverty, to pay for their bread a high price, in favour of the landlords.

It is a matter of the utmost importance not to place the House of Lords into direct antagonism with the Commons and with the masses of the people. Sir Robert says very correctly:

"I am afraid of other interests getting damaged in the struggle about the Corn Laws; already the system of promotion in the Army, the Game Laws, the Church, are getting attacked with the aid of the league."

FREE TRADE (1846).

Hansard

Source.—*Hansard*, Third Series, vol. lxxxiii., col. 276, June 27, 1846.

Sir R. PEEL: ... I fairly avow to you that in making this great reduction upon the import of articles, the produce and manufacture of foreign countries, I have no guarantee to give you that other countries will immediately follow our example. I give you that advantage in the argument. Wearied with our long and unavailing efforts to enter into satisfactory commercial treaties with other nations, we have resolved at length to consult our own interests, and not to punish those other countries for the wrong they do us in continuing their high duties upon the importation of our products and manufactures, by continuing high duties ourselves, encouraging unlawful trade. We have had no communication with any Foreign Government upon the subject of these reductions. We cannot promise that France will immediately make a corresponding reduction in her tariff. I cannot promise that Russia will prove her gratitude to us for our reduction of duty upon her tallow, by any diminution of her duties. You may, therefore, say, in opposition to the present plan, What is this superfluous liberality, that you are going to do away with all these duties, and yet you expect nothing in return? I may, perhaps, be told that many foreign countries, since the former relaxation of duties on our part—and that would be perfectly consistent with the fact—foreign countries which have benefited by our relaxations, have not followed our example; nay, have not only not followed our example, but have actually applied to the importation of British goods higher rates of duties than formerly. I quite admit it. I give you all the benefit of that argument. I rely upon that fact, as conclusive proof of the policy we are pursuing. It is a fact, that other countries have not followed our example, and have levied higher duties in some cases upon our goods. But what has been the result upon the amount of your exports? You have defied the regulations of these countries. Your export trade is greatly increased. Now why is that so? Partly because of your acting without wishing to avail yourselves of their assistance; partly because of the smuggler, not engaged by you, in so many continental countries, whom the strict regulations and the triple duties, which are to prevent any ingress of foreign goods, have raised up; and partly, perhaps, because these very precautions against the ingress of your commodities are a burden, and the taxation increasing the cost of production disqualify the foreigner from competing with you. But your exports, whatever be the tariffs of other countries, or however apparent the ingratitude with which they have treated you—your export trade has been constantly increasing. By the remission of your duties upon raw materials—by inciting your skill and industry—by competition with foreign goods, you have defied your competitors in foreign markets, and you have even been enabled to exclude them. Notwithstanding their hostile tariffs, the declared value of British exports has increased above £10,000,000 during the period which has elapsed since the relaxation of the duties on your part. I say, therefore, to you that these hostile tariffs, so far from being an objection to continuing your policy, are an argument in its favour. But, depend upon it, your example will ultimately prevail.... I do hope that the friends and lovers of peace between nations will derive material strength from the example which I have advised, by remitting the impediments to commercial intercourse. But observe, if that be the effect, I think in all probability that the continuance of permanent peace will expose us to more extensive and more formidable competition with foreign countries with respect to manufactures. During war we commanded the supply of nations. Peace has introduced not only new consumers, but also formidable manufacturing interests. In order that we may retain our pre-eminence it is of the greatest importance that we neglect no opportunity of securing to ourselves those advantages by which that pre-eminence can be alone secured. Sir, I firmly believe that abundance and cheapness of provisions is one of the constituents by which the continuance of manufacturing and commercial pre-eminence may be maintained. You may say the object of these observations is to flatter the love of gain, and administer merely to the desire of accumulating money. I advise this measure on no such ground. I believe that the accumulation of wealth, that is, the increase of capital, is a main element, or at least one of the chief means by which we can retain the eminence we have so long possessed. But I have attempted to show that abundance of provisions, and security (which is the main thing) for continued abundance, not only contributes to the accumulation of wealth, but that it is directly conducive to the alleviation of public burdens, by increasing the revenue; to the alleviation of local burdens, by diminishing crimes; but, above all, that it is conducive to the spread of morality, by diminishing those temptations to crime which arise from distress and poverty.... I cannot appeal to any ungenerous feeling—I cannot appeal to fear, or to anything which will be calculated to exercise an undue sway over the reason of those to whom these proposals are made. There may be agitation, but it is not one which has reached the great mass of the labouring classes, there being among them a total absence of all excitement. But this I do say—there has been a great change in the opinions of the great mass of the community with respect to the Corn Laws. There is between the master manufacturers and the operative classes a common conviction that did not prevail at 1842 or at a former period—that it will be for the public advantage that these laws should be repealed; and while there is that union of sentiment between them, there appears at the same time to be a general contentment and loyalty, and a confidence in your justice and impartiality.

Sir HOWARD DOUGLAS (member for Liverpool): ... This establishes, I think, the truth of what I had the honour of saying in this House on a former occasion: that there is a great difference between that plenty and low price which are produced by abundance of home production, and that which is produced by unlimited foreign importation; that the one quickens, the other deadens the home market; that

England is England's best customer; and that the contemporaneous exportation from England in return for foreign corn would be chiefly in British gold. Perfect free trade consists in the absence of restrictions on both sides.... We cannot combat rival tariffs, directly or indirectly, without subjecting British industry to severe depressions in relation to foreign industry and foreign labour.... To lay suitable duties upon the production of the foreigner, who lays burthens upon yours, does not give the monopoly of the home market to the home producer, nor turn towards any particular employment more capital and labour than would naturally go there. It only hinders that amount of those actually engaged from being turned away into a less natural direction. There cannot be two prices for the same article in the same market. The foreign consumer will not pay more for a British than for a domestic article of equal quality. The exporter cannot pay the rival duty, for, if so, he would sell at a loss or be undersold by the foreign rival: and therefore to compete with foreign protected markets British articles must be produced so much cheaper as to enter into this competition. The cost of production must therefore be reduced. This is most immediately and readily done by reducing the wages of labour, and it is most important to remark that it is precisely in times of pressure, when profits are most bare and labour most in want of employment, that this takes place and that mechanical labour is most extended. This not only displaces manual labour in times of pressure, but by so much precludes it from participating in future prosperity. It is difficult to trace the various uses of the money produced by the bills drawn on Great Britain by the exporters of foreign productions, for which they will not take British produce in return.... Whatever be the end of the circuitous transactions, the money payments made by us must first afford profitable investments to the rival interests of foreign nations and employment of foreign labour.... The noble lord, the member for the West Riding, observed forcibly, the increase of population requires additional means and sources of subsistence. But can we not find, do we not possess in our Colonies unbounded sources, rich fields of virgin fertility, from which we may derive unlimited supplies of British food? ... I have imagined that it might really be possible to treat the Colonies like counties of the country, not only in direct trade with the United Kingdom, but in commercial intercourse with each other, by free trade among ourselves, under a reasonable, moderate degree of protection from without, and so resolve the United Kingdom and all her Colonies and possessions into a commercial union such as might defy all rivalry and defeat all combinations. But free trade—the extinction of the protective principle, the repeal of the differential duties—would at once convert all our Colonies, in a commercial sense, into as many independent states. I defy any hon. member opposite to say that this would not be a virtual dissolution of the Colonial system. The British flag might still fly for a time, where sound British policy had raised it, in every part of the world. The colonists would regard it still with the veneration to which it is entitled. Our navies might still guard their coasts and waters and our troops hold military possession of their lands; but then would come the question of the economists, in debates on the Navy, Army, and Ordnance Estimates, What is the use of colonies? They consume not, as of old, the productions of the United Kingdom in any greater degree than if they were foreign States; we no longer consider and treat the colonies as domestic sources essential for the supply of the materials of our manufacturing industry and the elements of our maritime power; and it will be difficult to answer that economical argument, when, moreover, we shall have discarded our Colonies, for considerations of a wretched pecuniary economy, and sacrificed national objects and high destinies to the minor, and the comparatively mean, calculations of speculative wealth.

Mr. POULETT SCROPE: ... Sir, the plea of the weight of national taxation for a Corn Law appears to me not only a false, but a dishonest one. By no possible contrivance or juggle of protection can you fix the debt on the foreigner; it must still be paid by British subjects of some kind; and if you relieve yourselves from your share of it by any trickery of this kind, you can only do it by shifting the burden upon the rest of the community. You have chosen to place it on the most helpless of all the masses—the eaters of bread—who by your law must buy at your shop, at your artificial prices, and so pay the debt for you or starve. Is this right or is it wrong? No, sir, I repeat: if the Corn Laws do not raise the price of corn, they at least diminish its supply to a half-fed people. If they do, they can only benefit one class at the expense of every other. I take the speech of the hon. member for Northamptonshire, who may be considered to represent the pure protectionists. I appeal to the recollection of the House, if the main point of that speech was not an attack on what the hon. member called a stern dogma of a cold and hard political economy—viz., "that we should buy as cheap and sell as dear as we can"—a maxim which I would venture to call, not a dogma of political economy, but the very first principle of all commerce, the ABC of trade. But perhaps the hon. member despises trade and its shopkeeping maxims. But I am much mistaken if his friends and clients, the tenant farmers, act on any other than this vulgar and cruel mercantile principle themselves. They would not like to be compelled to act on the opposite principle of buying dear and selling cheap. No; what they really mean, and the hon. member too, in railing against the principle of buying cheap and selling dear is that the manufacturers should sell cheap to them, the farmers, while they sell dear to the manufacturers; and this is, in fact, the object aimed at by the Corn Laws. But the hon. member illustrated the cruelty of this flagitious dogma of a cold political economy by pathetic pictures, which were not without their effect on the feelings of the House. The first was that of a crowd of paper-stainers and silk-weavers thrown out of employment by the unpatriotic and anti-national preference of French silks and paper-hangings to those of British manufacture. Every picture has its reverse, and to the hon. member's picture of an ideal scene resulting from the operation of our mercantile principle, I will oppose a picture of the result of his protective principle, not drawn from the imagination, but one of the real scenes which did occur, in hundreds of instances, but a few years ago, in Paisley, in Stockport, in Manchester, and other places. Let the hon. member imagine a manufacturer at that time, his warehouses choked with goods which he could not dispose of; imagine that, after putting his workpeople first on low wages, next on half-work, he finally finds himself obliged to discharge them altogether, and to shut up his mill. They crowd in hundreds round him—a melancholy spectacle—men, women, and children imploring him for work and food. What is his answer? "All my capital lies locked up in yonder warehouses, and I have exhausted my credit likewise. The foreigner can buy no more of the goods you make because our laws prohibit his paying for them in the only thing he has to sell—his corn, the very food you want...." The hon. member does not seem to be aware of the fact that to buy anything from the foreigner we must sell to him something of equal value—that for every quarter of foreign corn or every piece of foreign silk imported we must expect to pay for it an equal value of goods the produce of our own manufacturers, and that British or native industry is as much employed in the one case as in the other, the only difference being (and a great difference it is) that by the free exchange we get more of what we want, or of a better quality, in return for our industry, than if we attempted to produce it at home. And this is just the benefit which commerce confers. The hon. member does not seem to be aware that the principle he declaims against as a cold dogma of a stern political economy is the one sole vivifying principle of all commerce, the stimulus to all improvement, the mainspring of civilisation—the principle, namely, of obtaining the largest and best result at the least cost; in other words, to get the most you can of what you want for your money or your labour. But I can hardly wonder at the opinions held by the hon. member, when I see him sitting on the same bench with the hon. member for Knaresborough, who abhors machinery as the root of all evil. It is a fitting alliance; in fact, it is the same fallacy in a different form. The notion that it is better to buy dear than to buy cheap is the same as that it is better to spend much labour than little to produce the same result. The idea is that the more of labour and capital anything costs to obtain it the better. So stated, it seems incredible that any man should entertain the idea. And yet this is the notion which lies at the bottom of all the declamations against machinery for economising labour and against the mercantile principle of economising capital. In both cases an increase of produce is obtained at a less cost, the very circumstance which alone raised the condition of civilised man above that of the savage.

PEEL'S DEFENCE OF HIS METHOD (1846).

Peel's Memoirs

Source.—*Memoirs by Sir R. Peel*, vol. ii., p. 318. (London: 1858.)

There are, I know, many who have freely admitted that a Minister was fully justified in the adoption of the measures of 1846, and who do not blame the resolution taken, but consider that some better mode of giving effect to it might have been devised—who are of opinion that a needless reserve was maintained towards a powerful party, and that a degree of irritation was thereby produced which more frank and unreserved communications would have prevented or mitigated.

I wish to give some explanation upon this point. I am the more desirous to give it because it was my intention—but for the unforeseen events of the autumn of 1845—to enter into that friendly communication, the omission of which is blamed and lamented, to apprise the Conservative party before the Corn Law could be discussed in the Session of 1846, that my views with regard to the policy of maintaining that law had undergone a change, and that I could no longer undertake as a Minister to resist a motion for the consideration of the whole question.

Had I been enabled to act upon this intention, I should, I presume, have fulfilled every obligation which party connections can impose, unless it be contended that a Minister may safely disregard the various circumstances which, even within a brief interval of time, may alter the character and position of many questions of public policy, and that, having once adopted a certain course, he is so committed to a blind perseverance in it that he must steel his mind against the influence of argument, the result of experience, the conviction of his own deliberate judgment.

That unreserved communication which I had thus contemplated—which is possible and most desirable under ordinary circumstances—was in this case unfortunately precluded by the peculiar character of the unforeseen emergency for which it was necessary to provide, and the peculiar position of the Cabinet in respect to the measures to be adopted.

There was no period between the first alarming indications of the failure of the potato crop, and the resignation of the Ministers on the 9th of December, 1845, at which I could with propriety have given the slightest intimation to the supporters of the Government with regard either to my own course or to the probable decision of the Cabinet. I could not have alluded to the differences which prevailed among the members of the Government without extinguishing whatever degree of hope there might be that those differences would be ultimately reconciled.

The course of events subsequently to the resignation of the Government on the 9th of December, equally precluded any confidential communication on my part with the supporters of the Government, which would have had a tendency to soothe irritated feelings, or to mitigate hostility to the measures about to be proposed.

It was a matter of public notoriety that the Government had resigned on the 9th of December, in consequence of differences on the subject of the Corn Laws—that Lord John Russell had attempted, and had failed in the attempt, to form a Government—that the Queen had thereupon appealed to her former servants, and that they had resumed power with the full intention of proposing measures with regard to the import of food to which Lord Stanley had refused to be a party.

To assemble the supporters of Government under such circumstances, for the mere purpose of communicating to them facts which were notorious to the whole world, would have given offence rather than have calmed irritation.

Had a meeting taken place, there would naturally have been the demand for a full explanation, not only of the grounds on which the decision of the Government had been taken, but of the peculiar character of the measures which it was intended to propose.

Explanation could not have been given on the first point without serious prejudice to the Government by anticipating the Parliamentary discussion which must shortly follow. It could not have been given on the second, namely, on the precise mode in which the duties on corn were to be dealt with, without disturbing all commercial operations connected with the corn trade, and incurring the risk of giving to some parties an unfair advantage over others.

There is no security against these evils in cases wherein the imposition or repeal of duties is concerned, excepting entire silence and reserve on the part of a Minister, until the hour when the intentions of the Government can be publicly declared in Parliament.

IRELAND: THE MOLLY MAGUIRES (1846).

Peel's Memoirs

Source.—*Memoirs by Sir Robert Peel*, vol. ii., p. 302.

Letter from Colonel Sir Charles O'Donnell to the Military Secretary, Dublin.

CAVAN,
June, 15, 1846.

Upon the whole, outrages have probably decreased both in number and in the seriousness of their character during the past period, and the general state of most of the country above-mentioned (Cavan, Leitrim, Roscommon, King's County, Westmeath, and Longford) may be considered tolerably peaceable; but in the wild parts of Leitrim and Roscommon, and their adjacent districts, the state of things is not altogether so satisfactory. Here Ribbonism is still in force; intimidation by means of threatening notices and visits from armed and disguised "Molly Maguires" is persevered in; waylaying, assaults, and robberies of arms and money take place; and all these arising, for the most part, from what is termed agrarian causes.

A man of the name of Donohue was, about the beginning of the month, fired at in the open day in the neighbourhood of Killeshandra, by several men, merely for having taken a farm in preference to another person, whose relative had previously held it. This man is marked for assassination, and will probably suffer.

A man and his wife, of the name of Tuthill, residing between Drummod and Ushill, were, on the morning (early) of the 7th instant, visited by a party of six men armed with guns and bayonets; and having beaten the husband till he was senseless, they stripped his wife, and placed her on her back over some fire which they raked out of the fireplace for the purpose. This was also for the same agrarian cause; and so intimidated are the sufferers that, although it is supposed they know perfectly well the perpetrators of the offence, they refrain from giving evidence.

Some few days ago, Bryan Kenny returning to Mullingar on a car, with a labouring man, while passing some cottages and a public-house, was fired at and wounded by a man who walked deliberately away unmolested by several persons who witnessed the event. Sir John Nugent had given Kenny some land, from which he had ejected another tenant for non-payment of rent; and though Sir John had given the ejected tenant compensation, and Kenny had paid him and taken a receipt for his "goodwill in full," the transaction was not considered satisfactory.

The day before yesterday, about 2 o'clock a.m., a party of nine or ten persons, some of them armed, went to the house of John Hazard, residing near Miltown.

On gaining entry by force they wounded the man's wife in the breast with a sharp instrument, and then, dragging Hazard outside, after beating him, endeavoured to induce him to swear he would not accept a situation as herd, from which another man had been dismissed.

Petty robberies and depredations continue to be committed in many parts of the country.

The Repeal movement goes on, but I have observed little energy with regard to it of late. Dissensions and mistrust are apparent amongst the members of this Association.

> [NOTE.— "Repeal" at this time generally meaning repeal of the Corn Laws, it should be remarked that in the above paragraph it means Repeal of the Union.]

ENGLAND AND THE YEAR OF REVOLUTION (1848).

Life of Palmerston

I.

Source.—*The Life of Lord Palmerston*, by the Hon. Evelyn Ashley, vol. i.,
p. 76. (London: 1876.)

A. *Lord Palmerston to Lord Normanby (British Ambassador in Paris).*   *February* 26.

What extraordinary and marvellous events you give an account of! It is like the five acts of a play, and has not taken up much more time. Strange that a King who owed his crown to a revolution brought about by royal blindness and obstinacy, should have lost it by exactly the same means, and he a man who had gone through all the vicissitudes of human existence, from the condition of a schoolmaster to the pomp of a throne; and still further that his overthrow should have been assisted by a minister deeply read in the records of history, and whose mind was not merely stored with the chronology of historical facts, but had extracted from their mass the reasons of events and the philosophy of their causes.

I can give you but provisional instructions. Continue at your post. Keep up unofficial and useful communication with the man who from hour to hour (I say not even from day to day) may have the direction of events, but commit us to no acknowledgment of any men, nor of any things. Our principles of action are to acknowledge whatever rule may be established with apparent prospect of permanency, but none other. We desire friendship and extended commercial intercourse with France, and peace between France and the rest of Europe. We will engage to prevent the rest of Europe from meddling with France, which indeed we are quite sure they have no intention of doing. The French rulers must engage to prevent France from assailing any part of the rest of Europe. Upon such a base our relations with France may be placed on a footing more friendly than they have been or were likely to be with Louis Philippe and Guizot.

B. *To Lord Westmorland, Ambassador at Berlin.*   *February* 29.

It must be owned that the prospect of a republic in France is far from agreeable; for such a Government would naturally be more likely to place peace in danger than a monarchy would be. But we must deal with things as they are, and not as we would wish to have them. These Paris events ought to serve, however, as a warning to the Prussian Government, and should induce them to set to work without delay to complete those constitutional institutions of which the King last year laid the foundations.

C. *To Lord Ponsonby, Ambassador at Vienna.*   *February 29.*

I should advise the Austrians to come to a good understanding with Sardinia as to mutual defence if attacked, which, however, they are not at present likely to be. But if the Austrian Government does not mitigate its system of coercion in Lombardy, and grant liberal institutions, they will have a revolt there; and if there shall be conflict in Lombardy between the troops and the public, and much bloodshed, it is to be feared that the French nation will break loose in spite of Lamartine's efforts to restrain them.

D. *To Lord Normanby.*   *April 11.*

Yesterday was a glorious day, the Waterloo of peace and order. They say there were upwards of one hundred thousand special constables—some put the number at two hundred and fifty thousand; but the streets were swarming with them, and men of all classes and ranks were blended together in defence of law and property. The Chartists made a poor figure, and did not muster more than fifteen thousand men on the common. Fergus was frightened out of his wits, and was made the happiest man in England at being told that the procession could not pass the bridges. The Chartists have found that the great bulk of the inhabitants of London are against them, and they will probably lie by for the present and watch for some more favourable moment.

E. *To Lord Ponsonby.*   *November 12.*

It is totally and absolutely impossible that Austria can keep quiet possession of the Italian provinces; and all you hear at Vienna to the contrary is nothing but the *bon à dire* of the Metternich school, and is the result of the established practice of the disciples of that school to go on asserting as facts that which they know to be false, but wish to be true, under the absurd notion that by frequent repetition falsehood may become truth. The only consequence of this system is that those who act upon it and those who are misled by it govern their conduct upon entirely erroneous data; and the results of such false policy are, that men like Metternich and Guizot meet in exile in London; that Sovereigns like Louis Philippe drink unwholesome water and sour small beer at Claremont, instead of champagne and claret at the Tuileries; and that ancient empires like Austria are thrown into anarchy and confusion, and are brought to the very verge of dissolution....

I quite understand the drift and meaning of Prince Windischgratz's message to our Queen, but pray make the Camarilla understand that, in a constitutional country like England, these things cannot answer; and that a foreign Government which places its reliance upon working upon the Court against the Government of this country is sure to be disappointed.

II.

Source.—*Letters of Queen Victoria, 1837-1861,* vol. ii., p. 221. (London: 1907.)

Queen Victoria to Lord John Russell.

Osborne, *July 25, 1848.*

The Queen must tell Lord John what she has repeatedly told Lord Palmerston, but without apparent effect, that the establishment of an *entente cordiale with the French Republic,* for the purpose of driving the Austrians out of *their dominions* in Italy, would be a *disgrace* to this country.... The notion of establishing a Venetian State under French guarantee is too absurd.

CONQUEST OF THE PUNJAB (1849).

Queen Victoria's Letters

Source.—*Letters of Queen Victoria*, 1837-1861, vol. ii., p. 257. (London: 1907.)

The Earl of Dalhousie to Queen Victoria.

Camp, Ferozepore, *March 24, 1849.*

The Governor-General is not without fear that he may have intruded too often of late upon your Majesty's time. But he is so satisfied of the extreme pleasure which your Majesty would experience on learning that the prisoners who were in the hands of the Sikhs, and especially the ladies and children, were once again safe in the British camp, that he would have ventured to convey to your Majesty that intelligence, even though he had not been able to add to it—as happily he can—the announcement of the surrender of the whole Khalsa army, and the end of the war with the Sikhs.

Major-General Gilbert pushed on rapidly in pursuit of the Sikhs, who were a few marches in front of him, carrying off our prisoners with them.

At Rawul Pindee, halfway between the Jhelum and Attock, the Sikh troops, as we have since heard, would go no further. They received no pay, they were starving, they had been beaten and were disheartened; and so they surrendered.

All the prisoners were brought safe into our camp. Forty-one pieces of artillery were given up. Chuther Singh and Shere Singh, with all the Sirdars, delivered their swords to General Gilbert in the presence of his officers; and the remains of the Sikh army, 16,000 strong, were marched into camp, by 1,000 at a time, and laid down their arms as they passed between the lines of the British troops.

Your Majesty may well imagine the pride with which British officers looked on such a scene, and witnessed this absolute subjection and humiliation of so powerful an enemy.

How deeply the humiliation was felt by the Sikhs themselves may be judged by the report which the officers who were present have made, that many of them, and especially the grim old Khalsas of Runjeet's time, exclaimed, as they threw their arms down upon the heap: "This day Runjeet Singh has died!"

CHARACTER OF SIR ROBERT PEEL (1850).

Greville Memoirs

Source.— *The Greville Memoirs*, 1837-1852, vol. iii., p. 349. (London: 1885.)

My acquaintance with Peel was slight and superficial. He scarcely lived at all in Society; he was reserved but cordial in his manner, had few intimate friends, and it may be doubted whether there was any person except his wife to whom he was in the habit of disclosing his thoughts, feelings, and intentions with entire frankness and freedom. In his private relations he was not merely irreproachable, but good, kind, and amiable. The remarkable decorum of his life, the domestic harmony and happiness he enjoyed, and the simplicity of his habits and demeanour, contributed largely, without doubt, to the estimation in which he was held. He was easy of access, courteous, and patient, and those who approached him generally left him gratified by his affability. The sacrifices he made upon two memorable occasions, upon both of which he acted solely with reference to the public good, forbid us to believe that he was ever influenced by any considerations but such as were honest and conscientious.... It is now impossible to fathom the depths of Peel's mind and to ascertain whether he had any doubts and misgivings, or whether he sincerely believed that Catholic Emancipation could be resisted and prevented. I do not see how he can be acquitted of insincerity, save at the expense of his sagacity and foresight. The truth is that he was hampered and perverted by his antecedents and by the seductive circumstances of his position....

It is almost impossible to discover what the process was by which he was gradually led to embrace the whole doctrine of free trade. We cannot distinguish what effect was made upon his mind by the reasoning and what by the organisation and agitation of the Anti-Corn-Law League. It may safely be assumed that, when he began to reorganise the Conservative party, he did not contemplate a Repeal of the Corn Laws, and that it was by a severely inductive process of study and meditation that he was gradually led to the conception and elaboration of that commercial system which the last years of his life were spent in carrying out. The modification, and possibly the ultimate Repeal of the Corn Laws must have formed part of that system, but what he hoped and intended probably was to bring round the minds of his party by degrees to the doctrines of free trade, and to conquer their repugnance to a great alteration of the Corn Laws, both by showing the imprudence of endeavouring to maintain them and by the gradual development of those countervailing advantages with which free trade was fraught. That, I believe, was his secret desire, hope, and expectation; and if the Irish famine had not deranged his plans and precipitated his measures, if more time had been afforded him, it is not impossible that his projects might have been realised....

He appears to have suffered dreadful pain during the three days which elapsed between his accident and his death. He was sensible, but scarcely ever spoke. Sir Benjamin Brodie says that he never saw any human frame so susceptible of pain, for his moral and physical organisation was one of exquisite sensibility. He was naturally a man of violent passions, over which he had learned to exercise an habitual restraint by vigorous efforts of reason and self-control. He was certainly a good, and in some respects a great, man; he had a true English spirit, and was an ardent lover of his country.

DON PACIFICO (1850).

Hansard

Source.—*Hansard.* Third Series, vol. cxii., col. 380.

[NOTE.—Although the resolution in the House of Lords against Lord Palmerston's action in regard to the claims of Mr. Finlay and M. Pacifico upon the Greek Government was confined to those matters, the resolution of confidence in the Government, which was moved in the House of Commons later as a rejoinder to the action of the Lords, was in general terms supporting the Government's foreign policy, so that Lord Palmerston was able to make his speech a wide defence of his policy.]

The resolution of the House of Lords involves the future as well as the past. It lays down for the future a principle of national policy which I consider totally incompatible with the interests, with the rights, with the honour, and with the dignity of the country, and at variance with the practice, not only of this, but of all other civilised countries in the world. The country is told that British subjects in foreign lands are entitled to nothing but the protection of the laws and tribunals of the land in which they happen to reside. The country is told that British subjects abroad must not look to their own country for protection, but must trust to that indifferent justice which they may happen to receive at the hands of the Government and tribunals of the country in which they may be.

Now, I deny that proposition, and I say it is a doctrine on which no British Minister ever yet has acted, and on which the people of England never will suffer any British Minister to act. Do I mean to say that British subjects abroad are to be above the law, or are to be taken out of the scope of the laws of the land in which they live? I mean no such thing; I contend for no such principle. Undoubtedly, in the first instance, British subjects are bound to have recourse for redress to the means which the law of the land affords them when that law is available for such purpose. It is only on a denial of justice or upon decisions manifestly unjust that the British Government should be called upon to interfere. But there may be cases in which no confidence can be placed in the tribunals, those tribunals being, from their composition and nature, not of a character to inspire any hope of obtaining justice from them....

We shall be told, perhaps, as we have already been told, that if the people of the country are liable to have heavy stones placed upon their breasts, and police officers to dance upon them; if they are liable to have their heads tied to their knees, and to be left for hours in that state; or to be swung like a pendulum, and to be bastinadoed as they swing, foreigners have no right to be better treated than the natives, and have no business to complain if the same things are practised upon them. We may be told this, but that is not my opinion, nor do I believe it is the opinion of any reasonable man. Then, I say, that in considering the cases of the Ionians, for whom we demanded reparation, the House must look at and consider what was the state of things in this respect in Greece; they must consider the practices that were going on, and the necessity of putting a stop to the extension of these abuses to British and Ionian subjects by demanding compensation, scarcely, indeed, more than nominal in some cases, but the granting of which would be an acknowledgment that such things should not be done towards us in future.

In discussing these cases, I am concerned to have to say that they appear to me to have been dealt with elsewhere in a spirit and in a tone which I think was neither befitting the persons concerning whom, nor the persons before whom, the discussion took place. It is often more convenient to treat matters with ridicule than with grave argument, and we have had serious things treated jocosely, and grave men kept in a roar of laughter for an hour together at the poverty of one sufferer, or at the miserable habitation of another, at the nationality of one injured man or the religion of another, as if because a man was poor, he might be bastinadoed and tortured with impunity, as if a man who was born in Scotland might be robbed without redress, or because a man is of the Jewish persuasion, he is fair game for any outrage. It is a true saying, and has often been repeated, that a very moderate share of human wisdom is sufficient for the guidance of human affairs. But there is another truth, equally indisputable, which is, that a man who aspires to govern mankind ought to bring to the task generous sentiments, compassionate sympathies, and noble and elevated thoughts....

With regard to our policy with respect to Italy, I utterly deny the charges that have been brought against us of having been the advocates, supporters, and encouragers of revolution. It has always been the fate of advocates of temperate reform and constitutional improvement to be run at as the fomenters of revolution. It is the easiest mode of putting them down; it is the received formula. It is the established practice of those who are the advocates of arbitrary government to say: "Never mind real revolutionists; we know how to deal with them. Your dangerous man is the moderate reformer; he is such a plausible man. The only way of getting rid of him is to set the world at him by calling him a revolutionist."

Now, there are revolutionists of two kinds in this world. In the first place, there are those violent, hot-headed, and unthinking men who fly to arms, who overthrow established Governments, and who recklessly, without regard to consequences and without measuring difficulties and comparing strength, deluge their country with blood, and draw down the greatest calamities on their fellow-countrymen. These are the revolutionists of one class. But there are revolutionists of another kind—blind-minded men who, animated by antiquated prejudices and daunted by ignorant apprehensions, dam up the current of human improvement until the irresistible pressure of accumulated discontent breaks down the opposing barriers, and overthrows and levels to the earth those very institutions which a timely application of renovating means would have rendered strong and lasting. Such revolutionists as these are the men who call us revolutionists....

The government of a great country like this is undoubtedly an object of fair and legitimate ambition to men of all shades of opinion. It is a noble thing to be allowed to guide the policy and to influence the destiny of such a country; and if ever it was an object of honourable ambition, more than ever must it be so at the moment at which I am speaking. For while we have seen the political earthquake rocking Europe from side to side—while we have seen thrones shaken, shattered, levelled, institutions overthrown and destroyed—while in almost every country of Europe the conflict of civil war has deluged the land with blood from the Atlantic to the Black Sea, from the Baltic to the Mediterranean, this country has presented a spectacle honourable to the people of England, and worthy of the admiration of mankind.

We have shown that liberty is compatible with order; that individual freedom is reconcilable with obedience to the law. We have shown the example of a nation in which every class of society accepts with cheerfulness the lot which Providence has assigned to it, while at the same time every individual of such class is constantly striving to raise himself in the social scale—not by injustice and wrong, not by violence and illegality, but by persevering good conduct and by the steady and energetic exertion of the moral and intellectual faculties with which his Creator has endowed him.... I maintain that the principles which can be traced through all our foreign transactions, as the guiding rule and directing spirit of our proceedings, are such as deserve approbation. I therefore fearlessly challenge the verdict which this House, as representing a political, a commercial, a constitutional country, is to give on the question now brought before it—whether the principles on which the foreign policy of Her Majesty's Government has been conducted, and the sense of duty which has led us to think ourselves bound to afford protection to our fellow-subjects abroad are proper and fitting guides for those who are charged with the government of England: and whether, as the Roman in days of old held himself free from indignity when he could say, "Civis Romanus sum," so also a British subject, in whatever land he may be, shall feel confident that the watchful eye and strong arm of England will protect him against injustice and wrong.

THE ROMAN CATHOLIC BISHOPRICS (1850).

Life of Palmerston

Source. —*The Life of Lord Palmerston*, by the Hon. Evelyn Ashley, vol. i., p. 245. (London: 1876.)

Lord Palmerston to his Brother.   January 27, 1851.

The Papal aggression question will give us some trouble, and give rise to stormy debates. Our difficulty will be to find out a measure which shall satisfy reasonable Protestants without violating those principles of liberal toleration which we are pledged to. I think we shall succeed. But all the newspaper stories of divisions in the Cabinet on this or any other question are pure inventions, wholly devoid of any foundation. The Pope, I hear, and the people about him by whom at present he is guided, affect to treat lightly the excitement which his measures have produced in this country, and they represent the clamour as a thing got up by the Church—a parson agitation. They deceive themselves; the feeling is general and intense all through the nation, and the sensible Catholics themselves lament what has been done.

The thing itself, in truth, is little or nothing, and does not justify the irritation. What has goaded the nation is the manner, insolent and ostentatious, in which it has been done. The Catholics have a right to organise their Church as they like; and if staff officers called Bishops were thought better than staff officers called Vicars-Apostolic, nobody would have remarked or objected to the change if it had been made quietly and only in the bosom of the Church. But what offended—and justly—all England, was the Pope's published Allocution and Wiseman's announcement of his new dignities; the first representing England as a land of benighted heathens; the second proclaiming that the Pope had parcelled out England into districts—a thing that only a Sovereign has a right to do—and that he, Wiseman, and others were sent, and to be sent to govern those territorial districts, with titles belonging thereto.

THE HAYNAU AFFAIR (1850).

Life of Palmerston

Source. — *The Life of Lord Palmerston*, by the Hon. Evelyn Ashley, vol. i., p. 239. (London: 1876.)

Lord Palmerston to Sir George Grey (Home Secretary). October 1, 1850.

Koller[2] is very reasonable about the Haynau affair.... I told Koller that it is much better that no prosecution should take place, because the defence of the accused would necessarily be a minute recapitulation of all the barbarities committed by Haynau in Italy and Hungary, and that would be more injurious to him and to Austria than any verdict obtained against the draymen could be satisfactory.

I must own that I think Haynau's coming here, without rhyme or reason, so soon after his Italian and Hungarian exploits, was a wanton insult to the people of this country, whose opinion of him had been so loudly proclaimed at public meetings and in all the newspapers. But the draymen were wrong in the particular course they adopted. Instead of striking him, which, however, by Koller's account, they did not do much, they ought to have tossed him in a blanket, rolled him in the kennel, and then sent him home in a cab, paying his fare to the hotel.

---

[2] Austrian ambassador in London.

PALMERSTON AND KOSSUTH (1851).

Life of Palmerston

Source.—*The Life of Lord John Russell*, by Spencer Walpole, vol. ii., p. 133.
(London: 1889.)

A. *Lord John Russell to Lord Palmerston.*

My dear Palmerston,—I must once more press upon you my views concerning an interview with Kossuth. I wrote to you some time ago that I hoped you would not see him. I wrote to you afterwards from Windsor Castle that I thought your seeing him would be improper and unnecessary.

I wrote to you again yesterday to say that I thought that, if upon his first arrival he had asked to see you to express through you his thanks to the Queen's Government for the efforts made by them for his safety and liberation, and you had at once seen him, it might have been thought a natural proceeding. But that, after his denunciations of two Sovereigns with whom the Queen is on terms of peace and amity, an interview with you would have a very different complexion.

The more I think on the matter, the more I am confirmed in this view.

It might have been right—although we did not think so—to interfere in the war waged by Russia in Hungary. But it cannot be right that any member of the Administration should give an implied sanction to an agitation, commenced by a foreign refugee, against Sovereigns in alliance with her Majesty.

I must therefore positively request that you will not receive Kossuth, and that, if you have appointed him to come to you, you will inform him that any communication must be in writing, and that you must decline to see him.

Yours faithfully,
J. Russell.

B. *Lord Palmerston's Reply.*

Panshanger, *October 30, 1851.*

My dear John Russell,—I have just received your letter of to-day, and am told your messenger waits for an answer. My reply, then, is immediate, and is, that there are limits to all things; that I do not choose to be dictated to as to who I may or may not receive in my own house; and that I shall use my own discretion on this matter. You will, of course, use yours as to the composition of your Government. I have not detained your messenger five minutes.

Yours sincerely,
PALMERSTON.

[NOTE.—In the end Lord Palmerston deferred to the wish of the Cabinet, and did not receive Kossuth.]

THE GREAT EXHIBITION (1851).

Life of Prince Consort

Source.—*The Life of the Prince Consort*, by Sir Theodore Martin, vol. ii., p. 247. (London: 1876.)

Extract from a Speech by the Prince Consort.

I conceive it to be the duty of every educated person closely to watch and study the time in which he lives, and, as far as in him lies, to add his humble mite of individual exertion to further the accomplishment of what he believes Providence to have ordained.

Nobody, however, who has paid any attention to the peculiar features of our present era, will doubt for a moment that we are living at a period of most wonderful transition, which tends rapidly to accomplish that great end, to which, indeed, all history points—the realisation of the unity of mankind. Not a unity which breaks down the limits and levels the peculiar characteristics of the different nations of the earth, but rather a unity, the result and product of those very national varieties and antagonistic qualities.

The distances which separated the different nations and parts of the globe are rapidly vanishing before the achievements of modern invention, and we can traverse them with incredible ease; the languages of all nations are known, and their acquirement placed within the reach of everybody; thought is communicated with the rapidity, and even by the power, of lightning. On the other hand, the great principle of the division of labour, which may be called the moving power of civilisation, is being extended to all branches of science, industry, and art.

Whilst formerly the greatest mental energies strove at universal knowledge, and that knowledge was confined to the few, now they are directed on specialities, and in these, again, even to the minutest points; but the knowledge acquired becomes at once the property of the community at large; for, whilst formerly discovery was wrapt in secrecy, the publicity of the present day causes that no sooner is a discovery or invention made than it is already improved upon and surpassed by competing efforts. The products of all quarters of the globe are placed at our disposal, and we have only to choose which is the best and the cheapest for our purposes, and the powers of production are intrusted to the stimulus of competition and capital.

So man is approaching a more complete fulfilment of that great and sacred mission which he has to perform in this world. His reason being created after the image of God, he has to use it to discover the laws by which the Almighty governs his creation, and, by making these laws his standard of action, to conquer nature to his use; himself a divine instrument.

Gentlemen, the Exhibition of 1851 is to give us a true test and a living picture of the point of development at which the whole of mankind has arrived in this great task, and a new starting-point from which all nations will be able to direct their further exertions.

I confidently hope that the first impression which the view of this vast collection will produce upon the spectator will be that of deep thankfulness to the Almighty for the blessings which he has bestowed upon us already here below; and the second, the conviction that they can only be realised in proportion to the help which we are prepared to render each other; therefore, only by peace, love, and ready assistance, not only between individuals, but between the nations of the earth.

PALMERSTON AND THE COUP D'ÉTAT (1851).

Life of Palmerston

I.

Source.—*The Life of Lord Palmerston*, by the Hon. Evelyn Ashley, vol. i., p. 289. (London: 1876.)

A. *Lord Palmerston to Lord Normanby (British Ambassador in Paris). December 3, 1851.*

My dear Normanby,—Even we here, who cannot be supposed to know as much as people at Paris did about what was going on among the Bourbonists, cannot be surprised that Louis Napoleon struck the blow at the time which he chose for it; for it is now well known here that the Duchess of Orleans was preparing to be called to Paris this week with her younger son to commence a new period of Orleans dynasty. Of course the President got an inkling of what was passing, and if it is true, as stated in our newspapers, that Changarnier was arrested at four o'clock in the morning in council with Thiers and others, there seems good reason to believe, what is also asserted, that the Burgraves[3] had a stroke prepared which was to be struck against the President that very day, and that, consequently, he acted on the principle that a good thrust is often the best parry.... As to respect for law and the Constitution which you say in your dispatch of yesterday is habitual to Englishmen, that respect belongs to just and equitable laws framed under a Constitution founded upon reason, and consecrated by its antiquity and by the memory of the long years of happiness which the nation has enjoyed under it, but it is scarcely a proper application of those feelings to require them to be directed to the day-before-yesterday tomfoolery which the scatter-brained heads of Marrast and Tocqueville invented for the torment and perplexity of the French nation....

I find I have written on two sheets by mistake; the blank leaf is an appropriate emblem of the present state of the French Constitution....

B. *The Same to the Same.*   *December 6, 1851.*

The great probability seems still to be, as it has, I think, all along been, that, in the conflict of opposing parties, Louis Napoleon would remain master of the field, and it would very much weaken our position at Paris, and be detrimental to British interests if Louis Napoleon, when he had achieved a triumph, should

---

[3] A nickname for the majority in the Assembly, comprising Thiers, Tocqueville, and others.

have reason to think that during the struggle the British representative took part (I mean by a manifestation of opinion) with his opponents. Now we are entitled to judge of that matter only by your despatches; and I am sure you will forgive me for making some observations on those which we have received this week. Your long despatch of Monday appeared to be a funeral oration over the President, with a passage thrown in as to his intentions to strike a *coup d'état* on a favourable opportunity, as if it were meant to justify the doom which was about to be pronounced upon him by the Burgrave majority. Your despatches since the event of Tuesday have been all hostile to Louis Napoleon, with very little information as to events. One of them consisted chiefly of a dissertation about Kossuth, which would have made a good article in the *Times* a fortnight ago; and another dwells chiefly upon a looking-glass broken in a club-house, and a piece of plaster brought down from the ceiling by musket shots during the street fights.

C. *Queen Victoria to the King of the Belgians.*

Windsor Castle, *December 23, 1851.*

My Dearest Uncle,—I have the great pleasure in announcing to you a piece of news which I know will give you as much satisfaction and relief as it does to us, and will do to the whole of the world. Lord Palmerston is no longer Foreign Secretary, and Lord Granville is already named his successor!! He had become of late really quite reckless, and in spite of the serious admonition and caution he received only on the 29th of November, and again at the beginning of December, he tells Walewsky that he *entirely* approves Louis Napoleon's *coup d'état*, when he had written to Lord Normanby by my and the Cabinet's desire that he (Lord Normanby) was to continue his diplomatic intercourse with the French Government, but to remain perfectly passive, and give no opinion.

II.

Source.—*The Life of Lord Palmerston*, by the Hon. Evelyn Ashley, vol. i., p. 316. (London: 1876.)

Lord Palmerston to his Brother. *January 22, 1852.*

As to the main point, John Russell distinctly narrowed down the ground of my dismissal to the fact of my having expressed an opinion on the *coup d'état* without reference to the nature of that opinion, Johnny saying that that was not the question. Now, that opinion of mine was expressed in conversation on Tuesday the 3rd; but on Wednesday the 4th, we had a small evening party at our house. At that party John Russell and Walewsky[4] were, and they had a conversation on the *coup d'état* in which Johnny expressed his opinion, which Walewsky tells me was in substance and result pretty nearly the same as what I had said the day before, though, as he observed, John Russell is not so "expansif" as I am; but further, on Friday the 6th, Walewsky dined at John Russell's and there met Lansdowne and Charles Wood; and in the course of that evening John Russell, Lansdowne, and Charles Wood all expressed their opinions on the *coup d'état*, and those opinions

---

[4] The French Ambassador in London.

were, if anything, rather more strongly favourable than mine had been.[5] More-over, Walewsky met Lord Grey riding in the Park, and Grey's opinion was like-wise expressed, and was to the same effect. It is obvious that the reason assigned for my dismissal was a mere pretext, eagerly caught at for want of any good rea-son. The real ground was a weak truckling to the hostile intrigues of the Orle-ans family, Austria, Russia, Saxony, and Bavaria, and in some degree also of the present Prussian Government. All these parties found their respective views and systems of policy thwarted by the course pursued by the British Government, and they thought that if they could remove the Minister they would change the policy. They had for a long time past effectually poisoned the mind of the Queen and the Prince against me, and John Russell giving way, rather encouraged than discoun-tenanced the desire of the Queen.

---

[5] Just before Lord Palmerston's dismissal was discussed in Parliament, Walewsky reminded Lord John Russell of these facts, and added that, whereas he had only conveyed Palmerston's opinion in a private letter to M. Turgot, he had made Russell's the subject of an official despatch. Lord John Russell asked whether Lord Palmerston knew all this, and meant to state it in the House of Commons (*Life of Palmerston*, ii. 326).

RELATIONS WITH RUSSIA (1853).

Life of Lord J. Russell

Source.—*Life of Lord John Russell*, by Spencer Walpole, vol. ii. (London: 1889.)

A. *Lord Aberdeen to Lord John Russell.*

I think that it will be necessary to be very careful in preparing instructions for Lord Stratford, if, as I presume, we must consider his memorandum as giving an outline of what he would desire.

"The assurances of prompt and effective aid on the approach of danger" given by us to the Porte would in all probability produce war. These barbarians hate us all, and would be delighted to take their chance of some advantage, by embroiling us with the other Powers of Christendom. It may be necessary to give them a moral support, and to endeavour to prolong their existence; but we ought to regard as the greatest misfortune any engagement which compelled us to take up arms for the Turks.

I do not believe that any Power, at this time, entertains the intention of overthrowing the Turkish Empire, but it is certainly true that any quarrel might lead to this event; or, as Lord Stratford says, it might take place without such a deliberate intention on the part of any one of these Powers.

We ought by all means to keep ourselves perfectly independent, and free to act as circumstances may require. Above all we ought not to trust the disposal of the Mediterranean fleet—which is peace or war—to the discretion of any man.

B. *Lord John Russell to Lord Clarendon.*   *March 20.*

The vast preparations at Sebastopol show a foregone purpose, and that purpose is, I fear, to extinguish the Turkish Empire.... My own opinion is that, in case of the invasion of Turkey by Russia on any pretence, we ought to send a message to Petersburg and *demand* the evacuation of the Turkish territory, and, in case of refusal, to enforce this demand both in the Baltic as well as in the Dardanelles.

We should, of course, enter into concert with France.

C. *Lord Aberdeen to Lord John Russell.*   *August 26.*

I always expected some difficulties to arise at Constantinople, but those which have taken place are very vexatious. We received yesterday a telegraphic despatch from Lord Stratford of the 19th, in which he said that the Turks proposed to make some modifications of the note sent by the four Powers for their acceptance....

They are not of great importance; but, after what the Emperor has already done, I doubt if he will accept them. At all events, after his prompt acceptance of our note, and his ready agreement to the alterations made by the English Government in the interests of the Porte, it is clear that we have no right to ask him.

D. *Memorandum by Lord John Russell for Lord Aberdeen, Lord Palmerston, and Lord Clarendon.* *September 3.*

Supposing the Emperor of Russia to agree to some of the amendments and reject others, there remains a fair ground for the conference to attempt a compromise. But, if he reject altogether the amended note, we must recur to the original pretexts of quarrel. The *pretence* of the Emperor of Russia was that his influence in behalf of the Greek Church in Turkey, as sanctioned by treaty and confirmed by long usage, had been treated with neglect. His *demand* was that concessions should be made to him such as could only be made as the fruit of a successful war.

E. *Sir James Graham to Lord John Russell.* *December 11.*

It is clear that his (Lord Palmerston's) part is taken; and that he hopes by raising the war-cry to drown the demand for an extension of the suffrage. This is the game which has been played before, and as you wisely foresee, is about to be played again.

F. *Lord John Russell's own account of the sleeping Cabinet.*

Mr. Kinglake has detailed, and has preserved in his fifth edition, a story regarding the dinner of the Cabinet at Pembroke Lodge, which, although accurate in the immediate purport of his relation, would give a very false impression of the real deliberations of the Cabinet. Some days before that dinner, a Cabinet meeting was held in the day-time, at which the whole question of sending an expedition to the Crimea ... was very carefully and very maturely discussed. Lord Palmerston for some months had been bent on sending an expedition to the Crimea, and I had only withheld my assent till the siege of Silistria should have been proved to be a failure.... Some days afterwards I gave a Cabinet dinner at Pembroke Lodge, and as the members of the Cabinet, with the exception of the Chancellor, had been present at the previous deliberation, they cared little for criticising after dinner the exact form of the sentences in which the number of the troops and the disposition of the fleet were minutely specified. It is no doubt true that several members of the Cabinet went to sleep during this discussion.

THE QUAKER DEPUTATION TO THE TSAR (1854).

Memoirs of Joseph Sturge

Source.—*Memoirs of Joseph Sturge*, by Henry Richard, p. 476. (London: 1864.)

At the appointed hour we repaired to the palace, and were received by the Emperor at a private interview, no one else being present excepting Baron Nicolay, who acted as interpreter, the Emperor speaking in French. After the address had been read by Joseph Sturge, and presented to the Emperor, the latter asked us to be seated on a sofa, while he took a chair, and entered into free conversation, kindly giving us a full opportunity for making any verbal statement that we might wish to offer. Joseph Sturge then proceeded to give expression to what had rested on his mind, not entering into the political matters involved in the dispute, but confining himself to the moral and religious aspects of the question. In the course of his observations he contrasted the Mohammedan religion (professed by the Turks), which avowedly justifies the employment of the sword, with the religion of Him whose reign was to be emphatically one of *peace*. He also remarked that among the multitude who would be the victims in the event of a European war, the greatest sufferers would probably be, not those who had caused the war, but innocent men, with their wives and children. On our thanking the Emperor for the kind reception he had given us, J. Sturge said, with much feeling, that although we should probably never see him again on this side of eternity, we wished him to know that there were those in England who desired his temporal and spiritual welfare as sincerely as his own subjects—when the Emperor shook hands with each of us very cordially, and, with eyes moistened with emotion, turned hastily away (apparently to conceal his feelings), saying, "My wife also wishes to see you." We were accordingly ushered into the Empress's apartment, where we spent a short time in conversation with her and her daughter, the Grand Duchess Olga, both of whom spoke English pretty well. The Empress said to us, "I have just seen the Emperor; the tears were in his eyes...."

The following is the substance of what the Emperor said in reply to the address. It was taken down immediately afterwards, and submitted to the revision of Baron Nicolay, who testified to its accuracy:

"I wish to offer some explanation of the circumstances which led to the present unhappy dispute. We received the blessings of Christianity from the Greek Empire, and this has established, and maintained ever since, a link of connection both moral and religious between Russia and that Power. The ties that have thus united the two countries have subsisted for 900 years, and were not severed by the conquest of Russia by the Tartars; and when, at a later period, our country succeeded in shaking off that yoke, and the Greek Empire, in its turn, fell under the sway of the Turks, we still continued to take a lively interest in the welfare of our co-religionists there: and when Russia became powerful enough to resist the Turks, and to dictate the terms of peace, we paid particular attention to the well-being of the Greek Church, and procured the insertion, in successive treaties, of most important articles in her favour. I have myself acted as my predecessors had done, and the Treaty of Adrianople, in 1829, was as explicit as the former were in this respect. Turkey, on her part, recognised this right of religious interference, and fulfilled her engagements until the last year or two, when, for the first time, she gave me reason to complain. I will not now advert to the parties who were her principal instigators on that occasion; suffice it to say that it became my duty to interfere, and to claim from Turkey the fulfilment of her engagements. My representations were pressing, but friendly, and I have every reason to believe that matters would soon have been settled if Turkey had not been induced by other parties to believe that I had ulterior objects in view; that I was aiming at conquest, aggrandisement, and the ruin of Turkey. I have solemnly disclaimed, and do now as solemnly disclaim, every such motive. I do not desire war; I abhor it as sincerely as you do, and am ready to forget the past, if only the opportunity be afforded me....”

    [The deputation was asked by the Emperor to postpone its departure, and was told by Baron Nicolay that the Emperor intended to send a formal reply to the address. Meanwhile the Duchess of Leuchtenberg, the widowed daughter of the Emperor, expressed a wish to see the deputation.]

“We called,” said Mr. Charleton, “at the palace of the Grand Duchess as proposed. But here our reception was very different from what it had been a few days before at the Imperial Palace. Instead of the earnest and cordial manner of the Emperor and Empress, the Grand Duchess received us with merely formal politeness. Her sorrowful air, and the depressed look of the gentleman in waiting, made it evident to us that a great change had come over the whole aspect of affairs. Nor were we at a loss to account for this change. *The mail from England had arrived*, with newspapers giving an account of the opening of Parliament and of the intensely warlike speeches in the House of Commons....”

But the respect shown to the deputation personally remained unabated.... The Emperor also sent a Government courier to accompany them on their return, with orders that everything should be done to contribute to the rapidity and comfort of their journey.

HORRORS OF THE CRIMEAN HOSPITALS (1854).

The Times

Source. — *The Times.*

VARNA, *August 20.*

It appears that, notwithstanding the exquisite beauty of the country around Aladyn, it is a hotbed of fever and dysentery. The same is true of Devno, which is called by the Turks "The Valley of Death"; and had we consulted the natives before we pitched our camps, we should assuredly never have gone either to Aladyn or Devno, notwithstanding the charms of their position or the temptations offered by the abundant supply of water, and by the adjacent woods. These meadows nurture the fever, the ague, dysentery and pestilence in their bosom — the lake and the stream exhale death, and at night fat unctuous vapours rise up fold after fold from the valleys, and creep up in the dark, and steal into the tent of the sleeper, and wrap him in their deadly embrace. So completely exhausted on last Thursday were the Brigade of Guards, these three thousand of the flower of England, that they had to make two marches in order to get over the distance from Aladyn to Varna, which is not more than ten miles. But that is not all. Their packs were carried for them. The ambulance corps has been completely crippled by the death of the drivers and men belonging to it.... Walking by the beach one sees some straw sticking up through the sand, and, scraping it away with his stick, he is horrified at bringing to light the face of a corpse, which has been deposited there with wisps of straw around it, a prey to dogs and vultures. Dead bodies rise up from the bottom of the harbour, and bob grimly round in the water, or float in from sea, and drift past the sickened gazers on board the ships — all buoyant, bolt upright, and hideous, in the sun.

SCUTARI, *October 9.*

Cholera and fever certainly have made great ravages since the departure from Varna, and the crowded state of the transports has prevented the men receiving the benefit which usually attends a sea voyage. Numbers arrived sickly and weak on the beach of Kalamita Bay, and the dreadful night of the 14th, during which the whole army stood knee-deep in mire, beneath a pouring rain, had an immediate effect on many who were comparatively healthy.... There is one experiment which has been a perfect failure. At the commencement of the war a plan was invented, and carried out, by which a number of Chelsea pensioners were sent out as an ambulance corps to attend on the sick. Whether it was a scheme for saving money by utilising the poor old men, or shortening the duration of their lives and pensions, it is difficult to say; but they have been found in practice rather to require nursing than to be able to nurse others.

SCUTARI, *October 12.*

It is with feelings of surprise and anger that the public will learn that no sufficient preparations have been made for the proper care of the wounded. Not only are there not sufficient surgeons—that, it might be urged, was unavoidable—not only are there no dressers or nurses—that might be a defect of system, for which no one is to blame; but what will be said when it is known that there is not even linen to make bandages for the wounded? After the troops have been six months in the country, there is no preparation for the commonest surgical operation. Not only are the men kept, in some cases, for a week without the hand of a medical man coming near their wounds—not only are they left to expire in agony, unheeded, and shaken off, though catching desperately at the surgeon whenever he makes his rounds through the fœtid ship, but now, when they are placed in the spacious building, it is found that the commonest appliances of a workhouse sickward are wanting.

October 18.

The manner in which the sick and wounded have been treated is worthy only of the savages of Dahomey. In one ship were four surgeons to 300 wounded and 170 cholera patients. Numbers arrived at Scutari without having been treated by a surgeon since they fell pierced by Russian bullets on the slopes of the Alma. The *Colombo* left the Crimea on a morning four days after the battle. She carried 27 wounded officers, 422 wounded soldiers, and 124 Russian prisoners, in all 573 souls. About half the wounded had received surgical assistance before they were put on board. To supply the wants of this mass of misery were four medical men, one of whom was the surgeon of the ship and sufficiently employed in looking after the crew. The upper deck became a mass of putridity; the neglected gun-shot wounds bred maggots, which infected the food on board; the officers were nearly overcome, and the captain made ill by the stench. Blankets to the number of 1,500 were spoilt and thrown overboard. Forty-six men were needlessly left on board two days after the arrival of the ship.

HEIGHTS OF THE ALMA, *October 20.*

When I was looking at the wounded men going off to-day, I could not see an English ambulance. Our men were sent to the sea, three miles distant, in jolting arabas or tedious litters. The French—I am tired of this disgraceful antithesis—had well-appointed covered hospital vans, to hold ten or twelve men, drawn by five mules.

THE CRISIS AT THE ALMA (1854).

The Times

Source. — *The Times*, October 10.

I. THE "TIMES" ACCOUNT.

Lord Raglan at last became weary of this inactivity—his spirit was up—he looked around, and saw men on whom he knew he might stake the honour and fate of Great Britain by his side, and anticipating a little, in a military point of view, the crisis of the action, he gave orders for our whole line to advance. Up rose these serried masses, and passing through a fearful shower of round, case-shot, and shell, they dashed into the Alma, and floundered through its waters, which were literally torn into foam by the deadly hail. At the other side of the river were a number of vineyards, and to our surprise they were occupied by Russian riflemen. Three of the staff were here shot down, but led by Lord Raglan in person the rest advanced, cheering on the men. Now came the turning point of the battle, in which Lord Raglan, by his sagacity and military skill, probably secured the victory at a smaller sacrifice than would have been otherwise the case. He dashed over the bridge, followed by his staff. From the road over it, under the Russian guns, he saw the state of the action. The British line, which had been ordered to advance, was struggling through the river and up the heights in masses, firm indeed, but mowed down by the murderous fire of the batteries, and by grape, round shot, shell, canister, case-shot, and musketry, from some of the guns of the central battery and from an immense and compact mass of the Russian infantry. Then came one of the most bloody and determined struggles in the annals of war. The Second Division, led by Sir D. Evans, in the most dashing manner crossed the stream on the right. The 7th Fusiliers, led by Colonel Yea, were swept down by fifties. The 55th, 30th, and 95th, led by Brigadier Pennefather, who was in the thickest of the fight, cheering on his men again and again, were checked indeed, but never drew back in their onward progress, which was marked by the fierce roll of Minié musketry, and Brigadier Adams with the 41st, 47th, and 49th bravely charged up the hill, and aided them in the battle.... Meantime the Guards, on the right of the Light Division, and the Brigade of Highlanders were storming the heights on the left. Their line was almost as regular as if they were in Hyde Park. Suddenly a tornado of round and grape rushed through from the terrible battery, and a roar of musketry from behind it thinned their front ranks by dozens. It was evident that we were just able to contend against the Russians, favoured as they were by a great position. At this very time an immense mass of Russian infantry were seen moving down towards the battery. They halted. It was the crisis of the day. Sharp, angular, and solid, they looked as if they were cut out of the solid rock. Lord Raglan saw the difficulties of the situation. He asked if it would be possible to get a couple of guns to bear on these masses. The reply was "Yes." The first shot missed, but the next and the next and the next cut through the ranks so cleanly and so keenly that a clear lane could be seen for a moment through the square. After a few rounds the square became broken, wavered to and fro, broke, and fled over the brow of the hill, leaving six or seven distinct lines of dead. This relieved our infantry of a deadly incubus, and they continued their magnificent and fearful progress up the hill. "Highlanders," said Sir C. Campbell ere they came to the charge, "don't pull your triggers till you're within a yard of the Russians." They charged, and well they obeyed their chieftain's wish. Sir Colin had his horse shot under him, but his men took the battery at a bound. The Russians rushed out and left multitudes of dead behind them. The Guards had stormed the right of the battery ere the Highlanders got into the left, and it is said the Scots Fusilier Guards were the first to enter.

II. A FOOTNOTE.

From a Private Letter from an Officer in the Guards.

We find that the whole garrison of Sebastopol were before us, under Menschikoff in person. His carriage has fallen into our hands, and in it a letter, stating that Sebastopol could hold out a long time against us; but that there was a position at the Alma which could hold out three weeks. We took it in three hours. So convinced were they of the impossibility of our taking it that ladies were actually there as spectators.

THE MORNING OF INKERMANN (1854).

The Times

Source.—*The Times*, November 24.

BEFORE SEBASTOPOL, *November 5.*

It had rained almost incessantly the night before, and the early morning gave no promise of any cessation of the heavy showers which had fallen for the previous four-and-twenty hours. Towards dawn a heavy fog settled down on the heights and valleys of Inkermann. The pickets and men on outlying posts were thoroughly saturated, and their arms were wet, despite their precautions; and it is scarcely to be wondered at if some of them were not as alert as sentries should be in face of an enemy. The fog and vapours of drifting rain were so thick, as morning broke, that one could scarcely see two yards before him. At four o'clock the bells of the churches in Sebastopol were heard ringing drearily through the cold night air, but the occurrence has been so usual that it provoked no particular attention. During the night, however, a sharp-eared sergeant on an outlying picket of the Light Division heard the sound of wheels in the valley below, as though they were approaching the position up the hill. He reported the circumstance, but it was supposed that the sound came from arabas or ammunition carts going into Sebastopol by the Inkermann road. No one suspected for a moment that enormous masses of Russians were creeping up the rugged sides of the height over the valley of Inkermann, on the undefended flank of the Second Division. There all was security and repose. Little did the slumbering troops in camp imagine that a subtle and indefatigable enemy were bringing into position an overwhelming artillery ready to play upon the tents at the first glimpse of daylight....

And now commenced the bloodiest struggle ever witnessed since war cursed the earth. It has been doubted by military historians if any enemy has ever stood a charge with the bayonet, but here the bayonet was often the only weapon employed in conflicts of the most obstinate and deadly character. The battle of Inkermann admits of no description. It was a series of dreadful deeds of daring, of sanguinary hand-to-hand fights, of despairing rallies, of desperate assaults, in glens and valleys, in brushwood glades and remote dells hidden from human eyes, and from which the conquerors, Russian or British, issued only to engage fresh foes.

"MUDDLING THROUGH" BEFORE SEBASTOPOL (1854-55).

The Times

I. THE "TIMES" ACCOUNT.

SCUTARI, January 4.

During the past week 1,900 sick have been brought down from the Crimea. A few cases of wounded men occur among them, but the vast majority are dysenteric. There are hundreds more at Balaclava waiting to be brought down.... One reason of the amount of sickness is the wet weather, which has interrupted the transport, even of commissariat supplies, between Balaclava and the camp, and which finds its way, not only through the men's worn-out greatcoats in the trenches, but (what is harder still to bear) through the rotten canvas of their tents. The consequence is that for weeks, whether in bed or out of it, they have hardly ever been dry. Their shoes, too, have been completely worn out, and they have had, thus wretchedly provided, to bear the exposure of the trenches for twelve hours out of the twenty-four, and wherever they went to paddle knee-deep in mud.

January 8.

Those who have been recently in the Crimea, and know the actual state of the army with respect to health, when you ask them the number of perfectly sound men left, reduce the already diminished strength of our battalions in a most startling manner. Diarrhœa and dysentery do not diminish either in the frequency or the intensity of their attacks. Since the last mail left we have had a snowstorm, and we know that the tents are still lying in Balaclava harbour without the means of transit. Mortification of the feet from exposure has for some time been an increasing feature of the cases brought down here. The army ought to have warm clothing by this time; it is humiliating to contrast the threadbare, tattered greatcoats, ragged trousers, and worn shoes of these poor sufferers with the serviceable, excellent uniforms of the Turkish army. What the army has had to endure in this way may no doubt in some degree be traced to the disgraceful manner in which for some years the clothing of regiments has been jobbed, but the more immediate cause of it will be found in a fatal mistake committed at the very outset of the Crimean invasion. When the troops landed, their kits were left behind to secure greater expedition on the march. On arriving at Balaclava, an order was issued to restore them, but no one had been appointed to take charge, and the consequence was that everybody in and about Balaclava was allowed to help himself.

II. EXTRACTS FROM OFFICERS' LETTERS.

Camp near Sebastopol, *December 28, 1854.*

The British army has suffered more from sickness than from the sword. Our men drag on in the trenches when they can scarcely stand. It is very wearisome trying to walk about for twelve hours in slush; the young hands cannot stand it. They sit down, get cramps, are carried to hospital, and die. The old soldiers know their only chance is to keep moving about.... Some arrangements must be made about firewood; there is none within two miles of us. We have no animals of any sort, or we might lay in a supply.

January 2.

A hundred or a thousand men, as the case may be, wet through and through, and up to the tips of their shakos in mud, sometimes without blankets, often without tents, take up their ground at a late hour, and there they lie. If they have something to eat, they are lucky. If they have not, they go without. Their frightful exposure brings on certain disease, and in a few days the dying and sick are the exclamation of every one. Lord Raglan (if Lord Raglan be really here, and not in London) is never seen.

January 4.

The contrast between the French organisation and the working of our own system is painful in the extreme. The French regiments all have their huts, instead of our decaying tents, and can at least keep dry when off duty. The streets of their camp are cleanly kept, and free of the intolerable mire of ours. Their transport was so well supplied from home that they have been able to bring up plenty of forage, with the result that they have kept alive a great number of horses, while we are reduced to a mere handful of beasts, which are stabled near Lord Raglan's quarters. We have hardly any animals to bring up supplies from the harbour, and none to fetch us firewood. The army has simply been deposited here by the people in London, and left to shift for itself. Have we any War Department at all?

January 12.

You will be surprised to hear me talk of hunger, but it is true. Our Commissariat is so badly organised that the men often have had no meat for twenty-four hours, often short supply even of biscuit and coffee. We are very badly off for fuel, the men having to go a long way for the most miserable twigs. Often we have had to march fatigue parties to port (Balaclava), some miles through mud, to bring up their rations in their haversacks—cruel work for men overworked in the trenches. Their boots are sucked off their feet in mud, they have no change of clothes, and how any man can stand it I know not.

III. FROM "THE MORNING HERALD."

Balaclava, *December 18.*

Along a flat, dirty causeway, rather below the level of the harbour, are boats and barges of all kinds, laden with biscuits, barrels of beef, pork, rum, bales of winter clothing, siege guns, boxes of Minié ammunition, piles of shell, trusses of hay, and sacks of barley and potatoes. These are landed in the wet, and stacked in the mud, until all the provisions that will spoil are sufficiently impregnated with both to be fit for issuing to the men. The motley crowd that is perpetually wading about among these piles of uneatable eatables is something beyond description. The very ragged, gaunt, hungry-looking men with matted beards and moustachios, features grimed with dirt, and torn great-coats stiff with layers of mud — these men are picked soldiers from our different regiments, strong men selected to carry up provisions for the rest of the camp. The rough, heavy-looking men in tarpaulin coats, sou'-wester caps, and high boots, are generally officers in the Guards. The very seedy-looking men in dilapidated garments, with bread-bags tied round their legs, are officers from the naval brigade; and so on.

THE ANGEL OF DEATH (1855).

Hansard

Source.—*Hansard*, Third Series, vol. cxxxvi., col. 1755.

Mr. John Bright: We are in this position, that for a month past, at least, there has been a chaos in the regions of Administration. Nothing can be more embarrassing—I had almost said nothing can be more humiliating—than the position which we offer to the country; and I am afraid that the knowledge of our position is not confined to the limits of these islands.

It will be admitted that we want a Government; that if the country is to be saved from the breakers which now surround it, there must be a Government; and it devolves upon the House of Commons to rise to the gravity of the occasion, and to support any man who is conscious of his responsibility, and who is honestly offering and endeavouring to deliver the country from the embarrassment in which we now find it. We are at war, and I shall not say one single sentence with regard to the policy of the war or its origin; and I know not that I shall say a single sentence with regard to the conduct of it; but the fact is that we are at war with the greatèst military Power, probably, of the world, and that we are carrying on our operations at a distance of 3,000 miles from home, and in the neighbourhood of the strongest fortifications of that great military Empire. I shall not stop to criticise—though it really invites me—the fact that some who have told us that we were in danger from the aggressions of that Empire, at the same time told us that that Empire was powerless for aggression, and also that it was impregnable to attack. By some means, however, the public have been alarmed as if that aggressive Power were unbounded, and they have been induced to undertake an expedition, as if the invasion of an impregnable country were a matter of holiday-making rather than of war.

But we are now in a peculiar position with regard to that war; for if I am not mistaken, at this very moment, terms have been agreed upon—agreed upon by the Cabinet of Lord Aberdeen; consented to by the noble Lord the member for Tiverton (Lord Palmerston) when he was in that Cabinet; and ratified and confirmed by him upon the formation of his own Government—and that those terms are now specifically known and understood; and that they have been offered to the Government with which this country is at war, and in conjunction with France and Austria—one, certainly, and the other supposed to be, an ally of this country. Now, those terms consist of four propositions, which I shall neither describe nor discuss, because they are known to the House;[6] but three of them are not matters of dispute; and with regard to the other, I think that the noble Lord, the member for the City of London (Lord John Russell) stated, upon a recent occasion, that it was involved in this proposition that the preponderant power of Russia in the Black Sea should cease, and that Russia had accepted it with that interpretation. Therefore, whatever difference arises is merely as to the mode in which that "preponderant power" shall be understood, or made to cease. Now there are some gentlemen not far from me—there are men who write in the public press—there are thousands of persons in the United Kingdom at this moment—and I learn with astonishment and dismay that there are persons even in that grave Assembly which we are not allowed to specify by a name in this House—who have entertained dreams, impracticable theories, expectations of vast European and Asiatic changes, of revived nationalities, and of a new map of Europe, if not of the world, as a result or an object of this war. And it is from these gentlemen that we have continually addressed to the noble Lord the member for Tiverton language which I cannot well understand. They call upon him to act, to carry on the war with vigour, and to prosecute enterprises which neither his Government nor any other Government has ever seriously entertained; but I would appeal to those gentlemen whether it does not become us—regarding the true interests and true honour of the country—if our Government have offered terms of peace to Russia, not to draw back from these terms, not to cause any unnecessary delay, not to adopt any subterfuge to prevent those terms being accepted, not to attempt shuffles of any kind, not to endeavour to insist upon harder terms, and thus make the approach of peace even more distant than it is at present? ...

I appeal to the noble Lord at the head of the Government and to this House; I am not now complaining of the war—I am not now complaining of the terms of peace, nor, indeed, of anything that has been done—but I wish to suggest to this House what, I believe, thousands and tens of thousands of the most educated and of the most Christian portion of the people of this country are feeling upon this subject, although, indeed, in the midst of a certain clamour in the country, they do not give public expression to their feelings. Your country is not in an advantageous state at this moment; from one end of the kingdom to the other there is a general collapse of industry. Those members of the House not intimately acquainted with the trade and commerce of the country do not fully comprehend our position as to the diminution of employment and the lessening of wages. An increase in the cost of living is finding its way to the homes and hearts of a vast number of the labouring population.

At the same time there is growing up—and, notwithstanding what some hon. members of this House may think of me, no man regrets it more than I do—a bitter and angry feeling against that class which has for a long period conducted the public affairs of this country. I like political changes when such changes are made as the result, not of passion, but of deliberation and reason. Changes so made are

[6] The four points were: (1) The protectorate of Russia over the five principalities was to be replaced by a collective guarantee; (2) the navigation of the mouths of the Danube was to be free; (3) the treaty of 1841, concerning Russia's position in the Black Sea, was to be revised; (4) Russia was to renounce all official protectorate over any of the Sultan's subjects.

safe, but changes made under the influence of violent exaggeration, or of the violent passions of public meetings, are not changes usually approved by this House or advantageous to the country. I cannot but notice, in speaking to gentlemen who sit on either side of this House, or in speaking to any one I meet between this House and any of those localities we frequent when this House is up—I cannot, I say, but notice that an uneasy feeling exists as to the news which may arrive by the very next mail from the East. I do not suppose that your troops are to be beaten in actual conflict with the foe, or that they will be driven into the sea; but I am certain that many homes in England in which there now exists a fond hope that the distant one may return—many such homes may be rendered desolate when the next mail shall arrive. The Angel of Death has been abroad throughout the land; you may almost hear the very beating of his wings. There is no one to sprinkle with blood the lintels and the sideposts of our doors, that he may spare and pass on; but he calls at the castle of the noble, the mansion of the wealthy, equally as at the cottage of the humble, and it is on behalf of all these classes that I make this solemn appeal.

I tell the noble Lord, that if he be ready honestly and frankly to endeavour, if possible, by the negotiations to be opened at Vienna, to put an end to this war, no word of mine, no vote of mine, will be given to shake his power for one single moment, or to change his position in this House. I am sure that the noble Lord is not inaccessible to appeals made to him from honest motives and with the deferential feeling that he has been for more than forty years a member of this House. The noble Lord, before I was born, sat upon the Treasury Bench, and he has devoted his life to the service of his country. He is no longer young, and his life has extended almost to the term allotted to man. I would ask, I would entreat the noble Lord to take a course which, when he looks back upon his whole political career—whatever he may therein find to be pleased with, whatever to regret—cannot but be a source of gratification. By adopting that course he would have the satisfaction of reflecting that, having obtained the laudable object of his ambition, having become the foremost subject of the Crown, the dispenser of, it may be, the destinies of his country, and the presiding genius in her councils—he had achieved a still higher and nobler ambition: that he had returned the sword to the scabbard—that at his word torrents of blood had ceased to flow—that he had restored tranquillity to Europe, and saved this country from the indescribable calamities of war.

WHY PEACE NEGOTIATIONS FAILED (1855).

Life of Lord J. Russell

Source. — *Life of Lord John Russell*, by Spencer Walpole, vol. ii., p. 263. (London: 1889.)

I was ready to incur the responsibility of advising the acceptance of the terms proposed in conjunction with the French Government. But I was not prepared to advise that we should depart from or even hazard our alliance with France for the chance of a peace on terms which I could not consider entirely satisfactory. Moreover, it was impossible for me to know the full weight of the motives which might have swayed the Emperor. The immediate result of our acceptance of the Austrian terms might have been the instant acquiescence of Russia, and the consequent evacuation of the Crimea. How would the French army have borne a retreat from before Sebastopol, relinquishing a siege which had cost so much blood and so much suffering? Might not the discontent of the army have disturbed the internal tranquillity of France, and even menaced the throne of the Emperor?

Lector House believes that a society develops through a two-fold approach of continuous learning and adaptation, which is derived from the study of classic literary works spread across the historic timeline of literature records. Therefore, we aim at reviving, repairing and redeveloping all those inaccessible or damaged but historically as well as culturally important literature across subjects so that the future generations may have an opportunity to study and learn from past works to embark upon a journey of creating a better future.

This book is a result of an effort made by Lector House towards making a contribution to the preservation and repair of original ancient works which might hold historical significance to the approach of continuous learning across subjects.

HAPPY READING & LEARNING!

LECTOR HOUSE LLP
E-MAIL: lectorpublishing@gmail.com